The Catholic Church Today: Western Europe. M. A. Fitzsimons, ed.

Contemporary Catholicism in the United States. Philip Gleason, ed.

The Major Works of Peter Chaadaev. Raymond T. McNally.

A Russian European: Paul Miliukov in Russian Politics. Thomas Riha.

A Search for Stability: U. S. Diplomacy Toward Nicaragua, 1925–1933. William Kamman.

Freedom and Authority in the West. George N. Shuster, ed.

Theory and Practice: History of a Concept from Aristotle to Marx. Nicholas Lobkowicz.

Coexistence: Communism and Its Practice in Bologna, 1945–1965. Robert H. Evans.

Marx and the Western World. Nicholas Lobkowicz, ed.

Argentina's Foreign Policy 1930–1962. Alberto A. Conil Paz and Gustavo E. Ferrari.

Italy after Fascism, A Political History, 1943–1965. Giuseppe Mammarella.

The Volunteer Army and Allied Intervention in South Russia 1917–1921. George A. Brinkley.

Peru and the United States, 1900–1962. James C. Carey.

Empire by Treaty: Britain and the Middle East in the Twentieth Century. M. A. Fitzsimons.

The USSR and the UN's Economic and Social Activities. Harold Karan Jacobson.

Chile and the United States: 1880–1962. Fredrick B. Pike.

East Central Europe and the World: Developments in the Post-Stalin Era. Stephen D. Kertesz, ed.

INTERNATIONAL STUDIES OF THE

COMMITTEE ON INTERNATIONAL RELATIONS

UNIVERSITY OF NOTRE DAME

The Overall Development of Chile

STUDIES IN
CHRISTIAN DEMOCRACY

VOLUME III

The Overall

Development of

Chile

MARIO ZAÑARTU, S.J., and
JOHN J. KENNEDY, *Editors*

CONTRIBUTORS
Mario Artaza • Tom E. Davis
Ricardo Ffrench-Davis • Federico G. Gil
Arnold Harberger • Henry A. Landsberger
Luis Scherz-García • Radomiro Tomić
Mario Zañartu, S.J.

UNIVERSITY OF NOTRE DAME PRESS
NOTRE DAME — LONDON

Library of Congress Catalog Card Number: 78-75152
Manufactured in the United States of America

CONTRIBUTORS

Mario Artaza is political advisor to the Chilean Embassy, Washington, D.C.

Tom E. Davis is chairman of the Department of Economics of Cornell University.

Ricardo Ffrench-Davis is with the research division of the Central Bank of Chile.

Federico G. Gil is Kenan Professor of Political Science at the University of North Carolina.

Arnold C. Harberger is chairman of the Department of Economics of the University of Chicago.

John J. Kennedy is chairman of the Department of Government and International Studies of the University of Notre Dame.

Henry A. Landsberger is professor of sociology at the University of North Carolina.

Luis Scherz-García is professor of sociology at the Catholic University of Chile.

Radomiro Tomić was formerly Ambassador of Chile to the United States.

Mario Zañartu, S. J., is professor of economics at the Catholic University of Chile.

PREFACE

Today Latin America is at an impasse. The facts of this are evident: the nations of Latin America are not developing at the required rate and social tensions are rising; such experiments as the Cuban Revolution and the approaches of the Alliance for Progress are not providing adequate answers to social and economic problems; democratic governments, at least in form, are disappearing in favor of military dictatorships.

Thus, republican forms of government along with authoritarian types (either military or one-party) have failed to move Latin American society. This difficult situation has naturally produced a search for other solutions that may provide more adequate answers to the problems. Chile under the leadership of the Christian Democratic party is trying to evolve something new and different in a final desperate effort to solve the impasse. If it fails, Chile will probably suffer a military coup d'etat or go the Marxist way of development. If it succeeds, success may mean a third way of development, one which could offer a more hopeful alternative for the whole of Latin America.

The essence of the third way of development is embodied in the so-called Revolution in Freedom. The Christian Democratic party wishes to engage the people of Chile in a genuine democracy, a democracy of participation. Under such a Revolution in Freedom intermediate organizations of the people would be more responsible for the economic, social, political, and cultural life of the country.

Such a third way has progressed more in its theoretical definition than in a successful practice. While it is important to analyze its theoretical content, the successes and failures of the applications of this program also must bear continual scrutiny. A

factual analysis of the first two years of the Revolution in Freedom is here provided. During the months since the material in
this book was prepared there have been no substantial changes
in the program. Some of the processes of change have been irre-
vocably consolidated in the areas of land reform, educational
reform, and political participation. In other areas aspects of the
program are still awaiting their initial implementation: labor
participation in economic decisions and intermediary organizations of the people. Others have temporarily failed: anti-inflationary plans and some development projects.

The analysis of the theoretical content of the Revolution in
Freedom was done by Chilean scholars largely familiar with the
United States academic world, while the analysis of the historical
background and actual practice of the Revolution in Freedom
was performed by American scholars largely familiar with the
current situation of Chile.

Mario Zañartu
John J. Kennedy

CONTENTS

Part I:

General Aspects

1: CHILE FACES HUMAN DEVELOPMENT

Radomiro Tomić

It is possible that the phenomenon that most decisively will affect the course of contemporary history may be the impulse to common standards of civilization that moves the people and the nations of what has been called "submerged Mankind." This growing pressure for a swift access to civilization is the Ariadne thread to what is happening in our times in nearly one hundred sovereign countries inhabited by 2.5 billion people on five continents, and what gives meaning to the deep ferment that stirs nations as old as China, as complex as India, as new as the thirty-five African states independent only since yesterday, and as similar and different as those of Latin America.

Undoubtedly the ideologies and methods through which they try to overcome the problems of underdevelopment are very different from one another. The surprising thing, nevertheless, is that in spite of so many differing ideologies and methods of approach, all of them tend so clearly to the same goal: a swift access to the instruments of action that define contemporary civilization.

Why analyze the case of Chile? In the first place, because it is a country that in a great measure represents the realities that are common to the other nineteen Latin American countries. Whatever the differences—and there are important ones!— among the nations of America south of the Rio Grande, it is necessary to remember that not without effect did they have during the first three hundred years of their history (with a certain license we could include Brazil) the same religion, the same language, the same king, the same laws, and the same administrators. The problems of underdevelopment in Chile are substantially identical in their nature and in their national and international projections to those of underdevelopment in other countries of Latin America.

Second, because for more than two years Chile has been carrying on an experiment whose basic purposes are to replace the present institutional and social order and to accelerate the integral development of the nation through a new, more dynamic social equilibrium.

The *ideology* is inspired by the values of Christian humanism of a nonconfessional projection. The *method* is the adherence to the spirit and forms of democracy. The *instrument of action* is the "will for change" that stirs the Chilean people, particularly the youth.

This Program was approved by the Chilean people with the highest majorities ever registered during the presidential election of 1964 and the congressional election of 1965. The motto was "Revolution in Freedom."

Is Revolution in Freedom possible in a country like Chile? Is it possible in a continent like America? In a world situation like today's? This is *the* question that must be answered within the next decade.

Let us, then, define the first question: What changes does *revolution* imply in a country with the cultural, historical, and social characteristics of Chile?

Revolution in Chile means replacing the present precarious social balance and its institutions by another scheme of national integration more representative and dynamic. It means the transfer of the effective centers of political and economic power from the control and service of the minority to the control and service of the majority. It means the ability to effect this transfer within the spirit and methods of democracy.

Theoretically speaking, three essential elements must combine to make social and institutional revolution possible.

First, an objective and subjective revolutionary situation must exist. To put it in other words, there must be a gross imbalance in the meaning the social order holds for the various groups that make up the nation and a certain degree of awareness of its inherent injustice by the social groups affected.

Second, there must also appear a revolutionary theory or ideology consistent enough not only to denounce the prevailing social order but to offer an alternative scheme to attain the national objectives proposed as indispensable for the community.

Third, there must be human groups sufficiently motivated, numerous, and organized to channel the driving force latent in the social imbalance that has been denounced.

Where these three elements combine—a revolutionary situation, a revolutionary thesis, and revolutionary forces in action— the efforts of the old order to quell it by dictatorial methods and force will inevitably terminate in a dilemma equally disastrous: either a violent and radically antidemocratic revolution or a degradation and abasement of the people, who cease to be a nation and sink into abject serfdom. We find examples of both in our own America.

For this *revolution* to take place in *freedom*, for it to take place within the framework of essential democracy, two complementary conditions must be added to those I have mentioned.

The context of the internal situation of a given country— Chile, in our example—must offer reasonable assurance that the minority will not flout by violence or arbitrary process the basic tenets of democracy by trying to deny to the majority the transfer of the levers of power.

The international situation must be favorable. Thus, the Revolution in Freedom must not provoke external antagonisms of such a nature that internal objectives have to be sacrificed to external security; nor, for want of an adequate measure of external solidarity, must it be compelled to strain the national effort to extremes that will not willingly be accepted by the majority for a prolonged period.

In short, Revolution in Freedom in Latin America today requires the concurrence of five elements. They are an objective and subjective revolutionary situation;

a revolutionary ideology that rationalizes the denunciation of the prevailing order and its replacement;

revolutionary forces with sufficient motivation and organization to mobilize the people, the youth, and the various sectors of the community with sufficient perception of the need and feasibility of social change;

a reasonably viable internal democratic context; and

a favorable international situation.

It is interesting to examine the case of Chile in the light of these requirements. Can it be said that a revolutionary situation exists in Chile? Is not Chile indeed the Latin American nation with the greatest stability and democratic continuity; the nation with an effective political freedom, suffrage, and organization; an effective freedom of press and speech, of protest and strike? At the same time, is not Chile first among the Latin American nations in the scope of its social welfare programs? Does it not rank second in literacy and fourth in a per-capita income that is almost equivalent to five hundred dollars a year?

Yes, this is all true, but closer scrutiny permits us to insist that the ineffectiveness of the prevailing social order and the imbalance and tensions it produces delineate a revolutionary situation in Chile that is objective and subjective.

In effect, after a century and a quarter of electoral tradition, only one Chilean out of every six had the right to vote in the 1958 presidential election. More than a quarter of a million school children were deprived of elementary education each year. The devastating effects of poverty determined a school dropout rate so high that only 2 percent of the students in the state university came from workers' homes.

Endemic inflation has so destroyed the value of currency, salaries, and social welfare benefits—at a rhythm that has constantly accelerated over the past thirty years—that the dollar today, in relation to the Chilean peso, is worth 6 times what it was worth in 1960; 60 times what it was worth in 1950; 240 times what it was worth in 1940; and 700 times what it was worth in 1930!

Our net economic growth between 1940 and 1964 was barely 2 percent a year, which is rather a negligible rate of increase on a 450 dollars per-capita basis. Ten percent of our population received more than half the national income. Five percent of our landowners held 75 percent of irrigated lands, and the *campesinos*, who constitute a third of Chile's population, were forced to subsist until 1964 on the equivalent of seventy-five cents a day *per family*.

Half of the population was homeless!

The lack of internal integration in Chile was so acute that our three main urban centers with less than 4 percent of the national area—Santiago, Valparaíso, and Concepción—accounted for 45 percent of the population of Chile, absorbed 75 percent of Chile's public health expenditures and 95 percent of investments in manufacturing and processing industries.

The profound sense of frustration that underlies our present society was dramatically expressed in the presidential elections of 1958 and 1964.

In 1958, in a contest involving four candidates, Senator Salvador Allende, candidate of the Communist and Socialist parties, won somewhat more than 29 percent of the votes. His opponent, Senator Jorge Alessandri, was elected with a little more than 31 percent of the votes. With less than 2 percent more of the votes the Marxist forces, with a platform of Marxist government, would legally have assumed the presidency of Chile in 1958. In that election the Christian Democratic candidate, Eduardo Frei, won 23 percent of the vote.

In 1964 there were three presidential candidates and 2.5 million people voted. Senator Frei was elected President with about 1.5 million votes, or 56 percent of the total. But there were a million Chileans who again voted for the Marxist platform espoused by candidate Senator Allende!

Are there revolutionary ideologies in Chile able to interpret this reality in a manner understandable by the large mass of Chileans and able to offer formulas for replacement of the existing order? Christian Democracy is one. Marxism is the other.

The first received the mandate of the Chilean people to convert into reality the revolutionary changes required by the integrated development of the nation. Therefore, what are the basic tenets of Christian Democracy and its Program of Revolution in Freedom?

In the first place, Christian Democracy holds that the *human person*, and not the state, or class, or race, is the supreme basis of society. The human person has essential rights that are inherent in his nature, that antedate the state and are superior to it, that cannot be sacrificed to any other consideration. The protection of these rights and the promotion of the full flowering of the individual person are the raison d'être of a social order.

It seems obvious that the social order prevailing in any country must be judged effective or inadequate, just or unjust, by virtue of the degree to which it effectively guarantees these essential rights of the human being and assures "the greatest good for the greatest number." "By your works shall you be judged. . . ." The semifeudal structures prevailing in underdeveloped countries ensure to only a small minority due respect for essential human rights, but they deny these same rights to millions of human beings conveniently called "the lower classes." The "lower classes," of course, are allowed to participate very feebly in the responsibilities and opportunities of the national destiny.

It might be well at this point to anticipate the hackneyed objection that historically the classic capitalistic system made possible the rapid capitalization and industrialization of Western Europe and the United States, particularly in the nineteenth century, when conditions produced for them what Walt Rostow has called "the takeoff."

That much is certain, to be sure, but it is equally certain that the accelerated formation of capital was obtained, particularly in Europe, on terms that cannot be repeated in Latin America in the second half of the twentieth century, and not for reasons of morality or principle alone. The capital formation was obtained at the price of imposing on the working masses for two or three generations such harsh and painful conditions of toil and life that are impossible to repeat, and was matched simultaneously by the ruthless exploitation of peoples subjected to the European soldier and merchant in Asia, Africa, and Latin America. Let us not forget that at the turn of this century Winston Churchill won a seat in Parliament by battling against the fifteen-hour working day. And let us not forget either that underdevelopment is the legacy left by colonialism in all countries that were subject to colonial exploitation. In regard to Latin America, underdevelopment is precisely the bitter fruit of not having replaced in time the traditional minority structures.

To those who say to us, "Do as we have done and you shall reap equal rewards," we must answer that history does not repeat itself. We must answer that today's circumstances differ radically from those of a century ago and that it is inconceivable that we should resort to the methods of capitalization used in the nineteenth century.

The Christian Democratic ideology holds forth to Chile a social order that can replace the individualist and Marxist-collectivist schemes. It is the *sociedad comunitaria* (communitarian society). The communitarian society, in our view, should be grounded in the following values and able to give them institutional being:

On the philosophical and moral plane the Christian Democratic ideology adheres—as I already said—to the principle that the human person as such, and not the state, or class, or race, is the supreme value in the community social order.

On the social plane the Christian Democratic ideology accords full support to the principle that to fulfill his destiny, the human person must simultaneously integrate organisms and social groups such as the family, the labor union and profession, the cooperative, the neighborhood, the municipality, the region, the political party, and the like. The communitarian society is a pluralistic society which can attain its own specific objectives only in terms of the existence and vitality of these intermediate organisms. In communitarian ideology a nation is formed, not by the mere grouping of millions of separate indi-

viduals who live within given frontiers, but by the orderly relationship and dynamism of those natural social groups without
which the development of the individual, and even his existence in itself, would be mere abstractions. There can be no personal destiny except through a pluralistic social organization
and structure. The state is the juridical expression of this fact
and its principal directive element.

On the political plane the communitarian society has to
be based on the dominant participation of the majorities in
the effective centers of power—social, economic, and political power—the control of which determines the national destiny. This has to be achieved within the spirit and practice of
democracy.

On the international plane the communitarian society asserts
the essential identity of the human race as a keystone for an
international order of peaceful coexistence among nations of
disparate political and social organization. It simultaneously
affirms respect for the national and cultural personalities of all
nations, and the need for multinational forms of political, economic, and social integration. It calls for the institutionalization,
as a duty, of the solidarity of the richer and more advanced
nations with those that are insufficiently developed.

On the economic plane the Christian Democratic concept
holds that while the communitarian society should evolve
toward communitarian ownership of the means of production,
it also accepts the legitimacy of parallel private and public
ownership. The accelerated development of the national economy has one of the highest priorities in an underdeveloped
society. The programming of this development is a function of
the public authority, but private enterprise has a substantial role
to play in its execution. The replacement of the private entrepreneur by the public *functionnaire* is not consistent with the
communitarian concept of the economy. But even more incon-
sistent would be the private capitalization of the toil and sweat
of others, or the private capitalization of the sacrifices made by
the nation or the community to speed its development. The

transfer to private pockets of public wealth is against the principles of Christian Democracy and thwarts the requirements of
its political scheme and its demands from the working masses.

The guiding principle here could be simply expressed: Private
capitalization of wealth produced by private efforts, private initiative, or private money. Capitalization by the community (which
does not always mean capitalization by the state!) of wealth
produced by efforts or sacrifices imposed on the community as
such, or generated by acts of public authority, or obtained
through the utilization of credit and other influences of the state.

What about foreign assistance and foreign private investments? A low level of savings, investment, and production; low
levels of education, technology, and information on world market possibilities—all typical of underdevelopment—spell the
need for a vigorous use of external technical and financial assistance, preferably from international organizations or public bilat-
eral sources, but also from selective foreign private investment.
Whenever possible, some form of association with national capital should be encouraged, to facilitate an organic integration
of foreign capital into the national economy.

It may be worthwhile to add to the definitions that distinguish the Christian Democratic ideology from the individualist
or the Marxist conception of man and society a complement in
the field of "tactics." We are conscious that Revolution in Freedom cannot accomplish more than what is possible within the
limitations, psychological and otherwise, of human nature.
The participation of the whole nation in the integral effort of
development requires clear, successive targets, freely accepted
and subject to periodical consultations with the people themselves or their representative organisms.

If it is true that nearly everything is possible for a sufficiently
united and motivated people—we could cite many dramatic
examples of this—it is also true that human nature has its inherent limitations. The process of revolutionary transformation
must not outstrip the bounds of a democratic majority con-

sensus or create states of tension so prolonged that they ultimately come into conflict with human nature.

For instance, we do not propose to create a *new and different* Chilean man, to eradicate the Chilean of today of his psychology, his mentality, his cultural heritage, and replace him by an entirely *new man*, possessed of another brain, another outlook, another culture, and another sense of values. That would be preposterous and totally unrealistic for a political purpose. Despite the centuries of brainwashing and subtle and brutal techniques that mark the history of man from the days of Pharoah Tutankhamen to those of Mao Tse-tung, the ancient, rich, complex, and contradictory nature of man always reasserts itself. Generous and petty at one and the same time; a mixture of saint and hero and villain and coward; capable, as St. Paul phrased it, "of seeing good, yet doing evil." And yet, capable also of subordinating his petty selfishness to the impulse to live for loftier and more exalted ends. It is then that he becomes capable of "moving mountains" and of transforming his world and the destiny of its peoples.

It is with this real and concrete man, this man of flesh and spirit, that the Revolution in Freedom concerns itself in Chile. Because we know this to be so, we do not bind ourselves to political dogmas of any kind. The transformation of the capitalistic and semifeudal Chilean social order of today into a communitarian society in which man and his rights become supreme can be accomplished only through the successive goals that the people establish for themselves by majority decision and on which they must periodically be consulted.

We have already mentioned the imbalance and contradictions that objectively shape a revolutionary situation. We have also mentioned the feeling of frustration and the will for change so clearly expressed by the people of Chile in the elections.

Which are in Chile the human groups able to unleash the latent revolutionary tensions? In a generic sense, the mobilization of a considerable sector of the people has already started.

However, it is interesting to be more specific about which are the groups that provided an active ferment and became the "spearhead" of this mobilization.

The first is youth as such, and very especially university youth. Contrary to what happens in other countries, the university students of Latin America are the "guard of honor," the shock troops in the battle for political freedom, for social justice, for renewal and change. There are those who believe that Latin American university students betray their specific duties in order to "play at politics" and at revolution. This is a shallow judgment. Reality is more profound and contains an element of anguish and urgency. The treason of older men is the one that forces the young to assume prematurely in our countries a role evaded by those who should do so because of their age, maturity, and social influence. If the social groups that have these responsibilities toward the nation and the community would effectively perform them, I do not think that the young generation of Latin America would feel as compelled to pay the price—often a high price of jail, ill-treatment, and blood—to become the "moral conscience" of their nation.

On the basis of time, the Chilean university youth were the first national group to be enrolled as a majority in the Christian Democratic movement. As far back as 1935 they provided the central integrating nucleus. In 1938 they assumed the responsibility of founding a new political party. In 1954, while the Christian-Democratic party had only succeeded in electing 5 representatives in a House of 147, and 1 senator in a Senate of 45, they obtained the highest majority in the elections of the student federation of the state university. Since then until now, for thirteen consecutive years Christian Democracy has been the overwhelming force in university politics, not only in the University of Chile, where half of the college students of the country receive their education, but in the seven other universities as well.

Important segments of the industrial proletariat, like the workers of the nitrate industry in the two provinces in the north of Chile, provided other earlier catalyzer cores (1941) of the feeling of frustration and popular discontent during the first years of the new party's life.

As time went on, the women of Chile began to accept and support the new ideas to such an extent that nowadays three women of every five vote for Christian Democracy, while only two men of every five do the same.

In recent years a very considerable proportion of the tens of thousands of families that in Chile—as in other countries of the world—surround the cities with a belt of poverty have increasingly begun to identify Christian Democracy with their painful struggle to obtain a piece of land on which to build their poor shacks, and to get schools, drinking water, sanitary systems, and so forth—and, what is more important, the sense that they belong to the nation and the nation belongs to them, too!

During recent years the rural masses that represent 30 percent of the Chilean population—almost 3 million of a total of 9 million—have begun to incorporate themselves into civic life and to come to a recognition of their security and social rights and to a consciousness of their human dignity, while they respond to the agrarian reform, the cooperative organizations, neighborhood committees, centers of mothers, and, in general, to the Christian Democratic Program for a new social order in Chile.

This brief description of the social forces that provide the energy of the Revolution in Freedom would not be fair or complete if I did not mention the determining role that a rather numerous group of professional men and other representatives of the intelligentsia of the country (some of them coming from old and traditional ranks) have played in the formation of the new political group, in its existence and development, and in the expression of its ideology and government program. Their high moral and intellectual qualifications have definitely contributed to the creation and consolidation of Christian Democracy in Chile.

We have already considered the first three elements of a revolution. But we have said that to achieve the substitution of a social order for another within the spirit and methods of democracy, two other elements are required: a viable national democratic context and a favorable international situation.

Is there in Chile a national context that allows for the possibility of a new social order within the frame of a democratic process? We believe there is, and some very significant data seem to prove it.

The long democratic tradition would be the first favorable factor. For more than a century and a quarter the Presidents of the Republic, the senators, representatives, and municipal officers, have taken office by means of elections held at the appointed time and, generally speaking, representing the electorate's will, even if it was a restricted electoral body.

The political abstention of the armed forces of Chile and their obedience to civil power is the second. During the final third of our century, Chile has successively had governments of the Right, of Popular Front, of Center-Left, of extreme Left, of extreme Right, and now a Christian Democratic government. Before these governments of such varied ideological and social tendencies the Chilean armed forces have maintained absolute abstention from the political life of the country.

Furthermore, by law since 1941 the armed forces assume the responsibilities of public order in all the national territory during election day. The law has entrusted to the honor of the armed forces the impartial guarantee that each party, each candidate, and each elector will be respected in their rights and civic options. The results have been so remarkable that not a single Chilean party would accept a change of this rule. I do not think a higher praise could be rendered to the civic spirit and the loyal dedication to professional duties on the part of the armed forces of Chile.

A third significant datum is the evident weakening of the traditional political groups in their political expression (today they only represent 15 percent of the electorate), as well as in their social influence, since they are swiftly losing the direct and indirect control of the rural masses. It is true that the new centers of financial and industrial power have a more decisive gravitation than what the landowners could exert during the last decades, but it is a fact that they do not constitute a monolithic block, that a policy of modernization of Chile offers prospects that are attractive to those entrepreneurs of a wider, progressive vision, and that although some industrial groups denounce the Christian Democratic policy of Chile, there in fact are others who support it.

A fourth favorable factor to crystallize the changes without breaking the democratic process would be the present spectrum of specifically political forces in Chile. It is true that we have unfortunately inherited the capacity that French politicians claim, to "divide a hair in four," and that for several decades, political life in Chile has been fragmented into too many parties. There were times when seventeen parties had representatives in Congress. Today in Chile there are seven political parties. Christian Democracy counts something less than 45 percent of the electorate; 25 percent goes to Marxist parties, 15 percent to Center parties, and 15 percent to the Right. In accordance with the proportional representation system, this voting percentage allowed Christian Democracy to obtain an absolute majority in the Chamber of Deputies in 1965 (82 deputies in 147). Because of the fact that in Chile, like in the United States, the Senate is only partially renewed at each election, in the 1965 elections only twenty of the forty-five Senate seats were disputed. Although Christian Democracy won twelve of those twenty seats, it only has a total of thirteen senators in a Senate of forty-five.

Although this distribution of forces in the Senate hinders the legislative process of the government, it does not make it entirely impossible in view of the ideological heterogeneity and the pragmatic antagonisms that divide the different groups of the opposition.

Finally, let us examine quickly the favorable set of international circumstances that provides the last factor which we have considered decisive for a Revolution in Freedom in Latin America in our time.

A favorable international situation is one in which the effects of the Revolution in Freedom in a given country do not produce an external antagonism strong enough to force this country to sacrifice the internal objectives of the revolution in favor of external security. On another ground, a favorable set of international circumstances is one in which it is possible for the program of Revolution in Freedom to depend upon the indispensable degree of external solidarity, so that the limits of the internal national efforts be compatible with the continuity of the democratic process.

Well, is there, then, a favorable international situation today? The positive signs are evident.

In the first place, we may note the manifest convergence between the objectives of the Revolution in Freedom and those of the Charter of Punta del Este of the Alliance for Progress. I am happy to point out that the government of the United States has given to the Christian Democratic government of Chile the greatest amounts of financial assistance in comparative terms within Latin America. In 1965 and 1966 Chile received slightly more than U.S.$16 per person a year through the various programs of the Alliance. That means at least three times more than was promised in 1961 at Punta del Este.

Furthermore, let us mark the complete coincidence between the Christian Democratic program of Latin American economic integration and the new forms of relationship that in this very field the ten countries of the Latin American Free Trade Association (LAFTA) and the five countries of the Central American Common Market are searching for.

Moreover, in spite of some spectacular breakdowns as occurred in the Dominican Republic, there is a slow but continuous improvement of the organization of American States' machinery for the peaceful and juridical solutions of conflicts within the continent. Notwithstanding some situations that still persist between Chile and some of her neighbors, the Chilean government has been able to spend only 9 percent of its budget for national defense. It is relevant to underline that this is one of the lowest percentages of the whole of Latin America.

Finally, whatever may be the minority interests slighted by the urgency of a swift and authentic democratization of the political and economic structures of Latin America, those who "have eyes to see and ears to hear" are becoming increasingly aware that President Kennedy was right when he hailed "the inevitable revolution" concept. President Johnson confirmed and accepted this concept on the fourth anniversary of the Alliance for Progress when he stated that this revolution in Latin America was not only inevitable but "indispensable."

We Chileans know very well that it is not for us to accelerate by a single minute the rhythm in which the new demands of history are expressing themselves in other Latin American countries. The "nonintervention policy in the internal affairs of other nations" is and will continue to be a cardinal principle of the foreign policy of Chile. We do not pretend, either, that what is valid for Chile should also be valid for all the other nations of Latin America. Revolution in Freedom is not an export item.

Nevertheless, the concern for urgently finding new forms of social integration, more stable and effective than the present ones, is alive and evident all over Latin America. Whatever the specific forms that the pressure for modernization, for broadening the democratic basis of social order, for incorporating the people into the responsibilities and advantages of the national destiny, may assume, such a tendency involves, not elements of antagonism, but of affinity and even of convergence with what the Chilean people intend to do within their own frontiers and in harmony with its own reality under the slogan of Revolution in Freedom.

What has been the meaning of Christian Democracy in Chile? What has been accomplished during the two years and five months under President Frei? Let us start from the beginning.

In October 1935 the initial nucleus of what was to become the Christian Democratic party was formed. In November 1938 it became an independent political party. In 1941 it elected its first two deputies. In 1949, its first senator. In 1963 in the municipal elections of that year it became the major political party of Chile with 24 percent of the electorate. In September 1964 its candidate, then Senator for Santiago, Eduardo Frei, was elected President of Chile with 56 percent of the votes, and in the congressional elections of March 1965, for the first time in more than one hundred years, a single political party obtained an absolute majority in the Chamber of Deputies and filled twelve of the twenty Senate seats in dispute—the Christian Democratic party.

Free of a priori dogmatisms, the ideological platform of the Christian Democratic party has been gradually developing in the context of the Chilean reality and of the experiences generated by political action in the heart of our people. I shall not allow myself to say that we have already found all the answers to the various problems that a change of structure, such as the one pursued by Chilean Christian Democracy, inevitably generates. On the contrary, with all objectivity and realism I can state that the ideological elaboration and the search for adequate solutions, even by trial and error, constantly continues.

Within the party, strongly united by a solid ideological platform, an intense and enriching doctrinal debate is under way, one related to the developing meaning and rhythm of the Revolution in Freedom and to the type of institutional structures more adequate to shape this stage of Chilean reality.

The government, on its side, has been able to carry out a substantial and, in several fields, an impressive part of the Program offered in 1964 and 1965. It has accomplished it without accepting ideological compromises and in spite of the implicit and explicit limitations derived from its scrupulous respect for democratic rules, which has enabled the opposition to prevent, postpone, or neutralize some important aspects of the Program.

The following indicate some of the basic aspects of the task that have been achieved.

1. Because of the determining participation of Christian Democracy in the Electoral Law Reform of 1963, the number of Chileans registered to vote has more than doubled, to increase the participation of the people in the generation of political power. A new, irreversible balance between the majority and the minority has been created in this fundamental aspect of the democratic process.

2. A powerful impulse has been given to education. Two hundred eighty thousand more children are now in school, to give Chile a school attendance of over 93 percent, a percentage comparable to that of Western Europe. There are nine thousand new school rooms and seven thousand new teachers; a million breakfasts and 400,000 free lunches every day are provided for children who cannot afford them. Sixteen thousand scholarships a year go to gifted students in secondary, professional, and technical education; three thousand university loans are made for higher education, loans to be refunded after students obtain the professional degree; 31,000 adult workers were trained in 1966 by the Department of Technical Assistance. Here are some of the most important facets of the gigantic impulse given by the Christian Democratic government to education in Chile during the last two years. And in our complex contemporary society *everything* starts with education, and nothing is possible—either for individuals or for nations—except through education.

3. The organization and incorporation of the rural masses is taking place. A third of Chileans—about 3 million people—live on and off the land. Until a few years ago their limited acquisitive power kept them practically outside the boundaries of the national economy; discriminatory legislation made it almost impossible for them to organize themselves in unions; the traditional system of property and farming concentrated 75 percent of the irrigated land in the hands of 5 percent of the landowners. Essential services like education, public health, and

security hardly reached the boundaries of rural life. Civilization in Chile, like in many other underdeveloped countries, did not reach much further than the last street lamps of the city. So it was before. But in an ever-increasing way this situation is changing.

In two years, even before the recent approval of the Agrarian Reform Law, more than 2 million acres (two-thirds privately owned) have been expropriated through legal process, and eighty *settlements* have been established, to give more rural workers land of their own than in the previous thirty-five years put together, and farmers are doubling and, in certain instances, tripling the former yield of this very land.

Two years ago there were in Chile only about a dozen rural unions with twelve hundred organized workers. Now there are more than one thousand unions and more than a hundred thousand organized workers belonging to them.

The wages of 1964—equivalent to seventy-five cents per family per day—have been doubled, and the rural family allowance has been more than doubled, thus to increase in a most remarkable way the demand for the consumer goods of the national industry.

With the Agrarian Reform Law, which is now in the last stages of the legislative process, the government intends to divide half of the irrigated land of the country, to create 100,000 new landowners, and to increase not only the volume of food production but also the productivity per man and per land unit as well.

It should be clearly understood that the inefficiency of the old order in the agricultural sector of the economy was really destroying Chile, economically, socially, and humanly, because while agricultural production has increased for the past thirty years at an average rate of 1.9 percent a year, the population growth has been at a rate of 2.5 percent a year. This is why while up to 1940 Chile was a net exporter of food, this balance has been altered in the opposite direction year after year. Now a fourth of the total amount of Chilean exports to the world has to be used to pay for food imported from abroad.

4. The organization of the community, meaning the basic social groups, is improving. Only through a concerted effort can people solve a substantial part of their daily problems, exert their proper influence on the national destiny, and participate creatively in an integral development program of the nation. Conscious of these realities, the Christian Democratic government encourages the Program called *Promoción Popular* in order to foster the organization of basic social groups in neighborhood committees, centers for mothers, cooperatives of all kinds, courses of professional and technical training, centers for arts and crafts training, as well as for cultural and artistic expression.

Promoción Popular has been founded, not with the purpose of having the state direct the people, but only and exclusively to give the people the *initial assistance*—professional, technical, and psychological—that is absolutely necessary to make the people aware of that basic wisdom: "Strength is in unity."

5. Half a million families without homes—and Chile is not a country of an easy tropical climate—was the heavy load inherited by the Christian Democratic government. The Program included the building of 360,000 homes for the period of 1964 to 1970. Although within the first two years eighty-five thousand homes were built—that is, the largest number ever built in national history—it is a fact that more urgent priorities in the utilization of limited available financial resources will force the government to reduce its housing plan to a maximum of 250,000 homes for the proposed period of six years.

6. In regard to health I shall give only three statistics. The number of medical cases treated by the National Health Service (*Servicio Nacional de Salud*) has increased from 7.8 million in 1964 to over 10 million last year. The distribution of milk has increased from 84 million liters per year to 188 million liters. And the death rate of children has decreased to an all-time low in national history.

We know very well that not only does the disease of under-development consist in the unfair distribution of wealth among the various social groups that form the nation but also—and this is even a more serious denouncement of the inefficiency of the old order—underdevelopment is a disease that makes the economy of a country a small one, an expensive one, and a very inefficient one. It means low levels of production, of consumption, of savings, of investment; continuous deterioration in a competitive market; and a growing dependency on foreign capital and foreign influence. That is why no real revolution is conceivable without economic development.

For this reason the Christian Democratic government offered a simultaneous program of social progress and economic growth. I have already pointed out some of the fundamental initiatives on the social plane. I would like to make a brief comment on what has been done and what we are doing to accelerate the economic development of Chile.

I want to start at the end: the increase attained in the national income per capita in 1965 and 1966. I realize that these figures reflect the effect of the Program and are not the Program itself, but they do reveal such dramatic effects that I cannot resist the temptation to start, as I said, at the end.

Increase of economic growth. We all know that the rate of economic growth is the universal norm whereby to measure the results of a development policy. Between 1950 and 1964 the Chilean economy increased at an average gross rate of a little more than 4 percent per year, while the population was increasing at an average of 2.5 percent per year. The net balance in the increase of goods and services had, for fifteen years, been below a net 2 percent per capita per year. Let us now compare!

In 1965 the increase in gross income was 7.3 percent, and practically the same figure holds for 1966. Upon deducting the increase of population, we find that in 1965 and 1966 the rate of economic growth per capita in Chile went up very nearly 5 percent per year, which is more than doubling and nearly trebling the previous rate.

Decrease of inflation. Devaluation of the currency in Chile had acquired a disastrous rhythm. In the twelve months before the advent of the new administration, the increase of the cost of living was 47 percent more than in 1963. Without a stable currency there are no stable wages, no social justice, no confidence in savings or investments, and no possibilities for a serious economic development program. The major difficulty for us stemmed from the fact that we were determined not to seek monetary stability at the expense of the working population or through deflationary measures.

This is not the place or the time to analyze in depth economic technicalities, but due to a combination of resoluteness, ability, and confidence of the nation, the rates of monetary devaluation were reduced to 26 percent in 1965, to 17 percent in 1966, and—we hope!—to 12 percent for the present year, 1967. These results were obtained simultaneously with a decided industrial expansion, with almost full employment, and with the dramatic advances recorded in the social development program which I have previously described. Could we call it a "little Chilean miracle?"

Program of agrarian and industrial expansion. Let me state some essential facts concerning such expansion.

Through the agrarian reform we are seeking not only a new and improved measure of social equilibrium, but also a new structure in farm production, in land and water use, that will allow an increase in the volume of food production and will raise productivity levels of the agricultural worker. The limited experience acquired in the last two years demonstrates that this is feasible.

However, independent of an agrarian reform which will affect only a segment of Chilean farmland, a vigorous program of agricultural promotion resulted already in 1966 in an increase of approximately 5 percent in the output of Chilean agriculture, as compared with a 1.9 percent annual rate of increase in the last thirty years.

To double the exports. Moreover, Chile is not predominantly an agricultural nation; it has a splendid basis for industrial development. It can easily be understood, therefore, that the new administration has undertaken a bold program to double Chilean exports in the next six years, to raise export levels from 500 million dollars in 1964 to 1 billion in 1970. To attain that objective, development plans contemplate a determined effort in special industries such as the production and refining of copper; iron ore and steel; wood pulp and paper; chemicals and petrochemicals; etc. Simultaneously, new laws creating incentives for exports and simplifying administrative red tape have been passed and are being implemented.

Without getting into details, I would like to tell you what has been achieved in only two years.

1. The volume of exports reached 900 million dollars in 1966 against 540 million in 1964.

2. Agreements with the large mining companies were negotiated to achieve the Chileanization of the copper industry, whose effects will be the investment of 530 millions of dollars, to double actual production between now and 1970, to treble the tonnage of copper to be refined in Chile, and to associate the government and the companies through the common ownership of the mines in some cases. It is a plan that at the present moment is being fully implemented.

3. To double the production of steel in Chile by increasing the output from 500,000 tons registered in 1964 to 1 million tons by 1969 through total investment figure which approximates the equivalent of 200 million dollars. The loans have been extended, and expansion plans are now proceeding ahead.

4. Two new cellulose pulp and paper plants are being built to take full advantage of the exceptional natural conditions of Chilean forest resources.

5. The same vigorous rhythm of expansion will apply to the production of energy and the electrification of the country through the full utilization of the gigantic hydroelectric potential stored in the rivers and lakes of the high Chilean Cordillera. Chile is already the Latin American country that has the high-

est rate of per-capita consumption of electric energy, and future expansion plans contemplate a more accelerated growth yet.

6. President Frei recently pointed out in a public speech that a survey of the 175 most important industries of the nation revealed that 140 are investing substantial amounts to increase their production capacity, while sixteen hundred applications to import machinery had been presented to the Central Bank of Chile.

Yes, the Revolution in Freedom knows that there cannot be any social development without a bold parallel program of economic development. Only in this manner will it be possible to substitute the sordid pattern of underdevelopment and to open the way for a new society possessing the standards of the twentieth century.

Foreign policy. There is still another fundamental subject that should be considered in giving an overall perspective of the Revolution in Freedom: How do we envisage the international order and Chilean foreign policy?

Christian Democracy maintains a vigorous stand on matters related especially to three spheres or subjects in the international field.

1. Latin American economic integration now, and its social and political integration in the future.

2. The whole of the inter-American system and the real nature and demands of the collaboration between the United States and Latin America.

3. The need to give political expression within the world order to the essential unity of the human race, to take advantage of the new possibilities brought by the stupendous advances of science and technology, and to use dynamically the obvious convergence of our days into a common type of civilization.

These are indeed fascinating subjects, but they cannot be treated or disposed of lightly. Their discussion must wait another occasion.

I have the feeling that perhaps my words are too assertive, even boastful, on what the Chilean people and Christian Democracy have been able to try and to achieve. If so, I present my apologies and request your indulgence. On the other hand, I can assure you that we have a keen sense of our limitations as individuals, as a political group, as a nation itself.

2: TOWARD AN OVERALL IDEOLOGY
OF DEVELOPMENT
Mario Zañartu, S.J.

Is it true that ideologies are dead? Is it true that ideological issues belong to the East? Is it true that time devoted to ideology is time lost for progress?

IS THERE ANY PLACE FOR IDEOLOGIES?

Where is the ideological concern in developed societies? What are the ideological issues at stake in the United States? Where are the ideological writers, the ideological schools, the ideological modelmakers, the ideological press, the ideological parties, the ideological labor unions, the ideological student unions of the United States? A few specks appear on the horizon.

It seems, too, that what underdeveloped countries should do is to face reality, not ideas, and put themselves to serious work; there is no substitute for hard work when development is at stake. Underdeveloped countries should have a greater political stability, more social discipline, better and more generalized education, and more interest in economic efficiency. They should stop their beg-the-rich policy as a solution to every single problem they are confronted with.

This seems true for all fields of human development, be they social, cultural, political, or economic. But it appears especially true when we are dealing with economic development, where the task is already well defined and the scientific progress greater. There is no place for ideological debates when you have to stop inflation, equilibriate your payments balance, guarantee the respect for investments, foster private initiative, protect private property, utilize the best economic techniques, interconnect markets, encourage savings, suppress barriers to trade, and so on.

The pragmatic approach, indebted to scientific and technical progress, has proved itself through trial and error in all developed countries. Why should Latin America, and Chile in particular, be an exception?

WHERE TO FIND THE IDEOLOGICAL ISSUES

Nothwithstanding, we think that progress in the developed countries does follow given ideologies, openly professed and operative in the so-called socialist countries, implicit in the so-called free countries. The underdeveloped countries (including Chile) are in their turn given developmental recipes which correspond to either one of these two ideologies.

And the different approaches are not due to simple matters of fact or divergent opinions. They are not just "bread-and-butter" issues. The differences in approach run more deeply than that. Thus, should nonintervention be the never-broken rule, or are there cases where some external power may intervene "to put order in the house"? When are such interventions right or wrong? Is success the only criterion for judging such interventions? Success according to what standards? Also, should nonpopular military governments, resulting from a coup d'etat and originating in anti-Communist fears and status-preserving concern, be backed in their developmental or anti-inflationary policies? What about providing them with military assistance? And, can the reasons given for or against the continuation of a war be brought down to "pragmatic" issues? Or can the approval or disapproval of the use of an internationally active youth organization by an espionage agency be decided on "practical" terms?

It seems to me that the above-mentioned examples are cases in point where the prevailing ideology in developed countries has not a ready-made answer. The fact that there is a dispute means that there is not just one answer, and the difference in the answers correspond exactly to the value structure of the persons or groups of persons implied in the issue. They might try to show how the solution sponsored by them corresponds better to the set of values prevailing in their country. What they are actually doing is looking after ideological consistency. They try to present solutions which are not in disagreement with the value system of their country as they comprehend it.

MISTAKES IN DEVELOPMENT ASSISTANCE

When dealing with developmental problems of other countries, planners from the developed nations propose recipes which have been successful in their own country. While this is natural, there is a danger of an ideology which may be native to the helping nation but alien, perhaps pernicious, to the country being assisted. The danger is a twofold one: (1) planners seldom make the necessary adaptations needed to fit the reality of underdeveloped countries, which is so different from their own; (2) they take it for granted that the general goals of development, be they political, social, or economic, and the priorities assigned to such goals, and the means to reach them, should be the same as in their society.

Their approaches will of course be completely different if they come from societies having different ideologies, like, for instance, one having a free enterprise system and another having a centralized system.

So, we have at least two sources of differences for the development policies recommended to underdeveloped countries by more developed nations. Some will support a free market; some will back government activity. Whereas the former will accuse the latter of creating a state oppressed kind of man, the latter will accuse the first of creating a rich-oppressed kind of poor. Both will fail for not giving enough consideration to the prevailing conditions of underdeveloped countries.

A DOUBLE IDEOLOGICAL CHOICE IS NEEDED FOR PROBLEM-SOLVING

Our task is twofold. Regarding ideologies, we have to decide what we want; regarding the situation, we have to find how to get it done. Ready-made recipes are not sufficient; they may fail either in their goals or in their efficiency.

Are our goals those of an individualistic, developed, Western society? Are they those of a collectivistic, developed, Eastern society? Or are they different from both? What are the priorities dictated by our own existing situation? We are clearly facing an ideological choice, and consequently, we must choose ideology when making such a choice.

Our development policy will to a large extent depend upon the answers to such questions. It will not be only a matter of pragmatic "bread-and-butter" issues or "trial-and-error" methods. Ideology will in many cases lead the way to finding new approaches and solutions which a "trial-and-error" pragmaticism could only reach at great cost, if at all.

IDEOLOGY DISCOVERS NEGLECTED PROBLEMS

The noted economist, Albert Hirschman, points to such a role of ideology when he speaks about what he calls the "stepchild" problems, those not calling attention to the established power centers. He says:

> Sometimes, as in Chile, rather elaborate theories were needed to forge a causal link between the privileged and the stepchild problems, and such theories will frequently have a strong ideological flavor. Here, then, is a useful, if latent, function of ideology which is so much in evidence in attempts at problem-solving in Latin America: ideology sometimes remedies the lack of direct access via

the construction of theories forging links between privileged and neglected problems.[1]

And the neglected problems have surfaced with the help of ideology. First, there are those that even an individualistic ideology was able to discover: the need for universal suffrage because of "equalitarianism"; the need for higher wages to establish mass consumption markets required by productivity criteria; the need for greater social mobility deriving from a desire to suppress extreme social tensions. Such developmental steps have not been taken through trial-and-error pragmatism only; they were derived from an ideological viewpoint, and then have been tried pragmatically.

Then there are all the developmental steps taken in accordance with a collectivistic ideology: suppression of private ownership of productive capital in order to prevent the exploitation of man by man; access to education for everyone as a means of providing equality of social opportunity; a totalitarian political organization in order to suppress opposition to, or a distortion of, the common good. Again such steps too did not result from a "trial-and-error" pragmatic development; they were all required by a given ideology.

Moreover, both ideologies may still fill other empty boxes in their systems. Their search for internal consistency may lead them to takes new steps, to discover hidden "stepchild" problems and focus attention upon them.

PROBLEMS DISCOVERED BY COMMUNITARIAN IDEOLOGY

However it can still be argued that in all preceding cases, because they are all steps already taken, it is not clear whether ideological pressure preceded or was a result of trial-and-error pragmatism.

But discussion becomes impossible when dealing with ideologies which in large measure have not yet had their practicality tested because they have not possessed, at least not for a long

[1] Albert O. Hirschman, *Journal Toward Progress* (New York: The Twentieth Century Fund, 1963), p. 231.

period of time, economic, social, or political power. Such is the case of communitarian ideology, which has not been tested so far, and which is an application to underdeveloped countries of the "personalist," "humanistic," "democratic," or "Christian social" doctrinal approach to man and society.

Since such an ideology has not been tested, it cannot be said that the steps it sponsors, independent and different from the existing situation, are a result of trial and error. Such is the case of such communitarian formulae as "*Promoción Popular*" for social development, "communitarian enterprise" for economic development, and "Revolution in Freedom" for political development. They have never been tested, they are different from the existing situation, they are an unavoidable requirement of ideological consistency, and they are being strongly proclaimed by communitarianists. Their first trial pragmatic test is being started in Chile, where they have acceded to political power.

The well-founded criticism made by Desal to the Alliance for Progress was not a result of trial and error; it was an ideological criticism which was able to call attention to a basic shortcoming of the Alliance: it could not attain its goals because it was a "government-to-government" rather than a "people-to-people" alliance; people were considered, not as active and responsible agents, but as "object," beneficiaries of development. Only an ideological agency concerned with the people's active participation in the process of Latin American development could so quickly, and so independently of trial-and-error pragmatic checks, be able to detect a basic shortcoming in this aspect.

The preceding considerations tended to prove the point that ideologies may have a very important role in the process of development.

ROLE OF IDEOLOGY IN EXPLANATION AND CURE OF PROBLEMS

Even in explaining the reasons for backwardness of countries we are focusing successively on a number of different explanations, each of which leads to the espousal of certain policies and positions on overall developmental problems; "in other words," says Hirschman, "each determines a 'system,' is part of an ideology"; he continues:

> We need not go all the way with Keynes' dictum that "the world is ruled by little else" than by the ideas, both the right and the wrong ones, of economists and political philosophers to recognize the importance of these ideas for the shaping of reality. Yet, the subject is strangely neglected. We are far better informed about changes in the balance of payments, terms of trade, capital formation, etc., of foreign countries than about the climate of opinion, the alignment of contending economic theories on policy issues, or about the emergence of new reform proposals. When we are called upon to advise a Latin American country on economic policy, it is only natural that, hard pressed, we should first of all attempt to get at the "facts," a difficult enough undertaking. But frequently our advice would be futile unless we have also gained an understanding of the understanding Latin Americans have of their own reality.
>
> A better knowledge of Latin American economic ideas seems particularly important at this time. Rapid political and social changes in the area lead to the sudden appearance of new leaders. Without much experience in the handling of public affairs and with a strong desire quickly to solve their country's problems, they are apt to reach out for the ready-made policy prescriptions of various ideologies.[2]

ALLEGED REASONS TO DISTRUST IDEOLOGIES

How to explain, then, this kind of instinctive animadversion against ideologies prevailing in some of the most developed countries? There seems to be reasons for such distrust. First of all, many times utopian solutions to problems seem to be the result of ideological concerns; this has been true in regard to

[2] Albert O. Hirschman, ed., *Latin American Issues* (New York: Twentieth Century Fund, 1961), pp. 3-4.

many a candid socialist in the nonsocialist countries or for many a laissez-faire follower in the nondeveloped countries. But the question comes, Is this due to the ideological concern or is it rather due to an insufficient concern about the real situation? It seems that the right explanation is rather the last one: insufficient concern about the real situation. Such concern cannot be substituted for, but it is not by itself always sufficient to solve the problems.

Then there is the experience and the fear that ideological concern will bring about ideological disputes, and therefore unneeded and troublesome divisions in society; stones will be thrown between free enterprisers and government planners, between conservatives and revolutionaries, between authoritarianists and democrats. Is it not less divisionist to face each problem on its own merits and propose pragmatic solutions? It is certainly true that many times ideologists seem to fight over issues having no more than one viable solution. But either problems have more than one solution or there is more than one way to implement a given solution. If such is the case, what will be the criteria whereby to make a choice? In other words, an ideological choice is being required. The fact that such a choice and the disputes over it mean divisions is really a tautology; it would be more correct to say that the existing division of society becomes manifest also when developmental problems are faced. The only ways to surpress such disputes are either to have a monolithic ideology or to have one of many ideologies (either native or alien) impose its own approach on the rest of them.

Finally, it is said that ideologies do not solve the real problems, that they are impractical and remain in the heaven of ideas only, when what is needed are practical steps to be taken toward development. Ideologies seem, therefore, not to be of much help for problem-solving. And this is true because ideology is not everything. For one thing it does not provide by itself the practical steps to be taken. If a social reform movement stays only at this stage of human activity, it will certainly not be operative, and it will be unable to change or to accomplish anything. But if we consider ideology as one of the necessary steps toward action, we are not saying we should remain there. The selection of means and mechanisms, and their actual being put into practice, are also necessary steps toward action, and no social reform movement can dispense with them. However, no movement can dispense with the choice of priority goals to be attained through such means and mechanisms; in other words, it cannot dispense with ideology.

Now in regard to the situation of Latin America, and more specifically to the Chilean situation, is there any reason why ideologies should be explicit in the process of overall development?

NEED FOR EXPLICIT IDEOLOGY IN DEVELOPING COUNTRIES

The question now is not whether or not there should be an ideology of overall development. There is no doubt about it. The question is whether such ideology should be implicit or explicit, whether or not it should be explicit even in some of the institutions of change, such as labor or student unions, or political parties.

There seems to be only one possibility of Chilean overall development not having an explicit ideology. Such a possibility is that all the Chilean people agree on either the individualistic or the collectivistic ideology of developed countries, and that the Chilean situation be such as not to require any change for the application of the ideological recipes.

But in fact, nobody would hold that the Chilean situation can be treated with foreign recipes not adapted to its needs. This is one reason for new ideological approaches. But also it can hardly be maintained that the majority of Chileans are favorable either to individualistic or collectivistic ideology. The majority, according to polls and sociological surveys, seem to be increasingly in favor of this new ideology we have called communitarianism. If this is true, the development "problem-solving" process has to be subjected to such an ideological choice.

But this reasoning may only justify the existence of a few research centers, be it at the doctrinal, the ideological or the political level, where the practical steps to be undertaken and the institutions to be created are defined, and their implementation passed over to the decision-makers and propaganda apparatus. Why should some of the institutions themselves be ideologically oriented? Why should there be Christian Democratic parties, Christian labor unions, Social Christian revolutionary students' unions, and the like? Why not just Democratic party, labor union, and national student union?

The reason is that at the first steps of development institutions are not specific enough; there is not a variety of institutions rich enough to care specifically about every aspect of social life, and there is therefore for every one of the existing institutions a broader task than its title would indicate: student unions are not just student unions; they are also somehow political bodies, social pressure groups, cultural elites, revolutionary and protest movements. Similarly, labor unions are not just labor unions; they also are political bodies, social pressure groups, economic power, revolutionary and protest movements. And political parties are not just political parties; they also are employment agencies, social mobility agents, training centers, community organizations, and either conservative or revolutionary movements.

We are conscious of the fact that this is not an ideal situation; that in order to be efficient, institutions have to be specific; that development implies a network of specific institutions. But the fact is that our society is underdeveloped and that therefore our institutions are few and nonspecific. Development will consist in institutions becoming more and more specific and therefore less and less ideological. But such developed institutional model is still way ahead. In our present situation we have to count on multipurpose institutions of a nonspecific character.

But why should such multipurpose institutions be ideologically oriented? First, because there are no international models of multipurpose institutions fitting our own circumstances. Second, because if there were, they would pursue ideologies different from our own. And third, because people in our countures demand that *the*, or *the few*, institutions which serve them present them with an explicit idea of man and society and related problems. Not to be explicitly oriented ideologically would mean for these multipurpose institutions, undergoing a process of communitarian revolution, either to fail in facing the real situation or to serve alternative ideologies: individualistic or collectivistic.

DEFINITIONS OF IDEOLOGY

Before proceeding any further it is necessary to give a precise definition of what we are talking about: ideology and overall development.

In its current use the term "ideology" is applied to a development process means a relatively consistent body of values, ideas, or propositions, tested or untested, aiming at explaining underdevelopment and at indicating its cure.

But under such a meaning many things are covered, like for instance every development policy, doctrine, plan, or strategy. It is necessary to try to define more closely what we will label ideology. We all agree on what is called a social philosophy, a philosophy of man and society, which necessarily comprehends a personal and social ethic. When we try to involve a consideration of reality as it appears to us through positive science and technology in our ethical judgments, we abandon the field of pure ethics and are already moving in the field of doctrine, in the sense we use the word when saying Christian social doctrine, individualistic doctrine, or Marxist doctrine. Taken in such a sense, doctrines cover all aspects of the life of man in society, and produce an infinite quantity of models for the solution of any possible problem of life, be it personal or institutional.

Doctrines do not by themselves establish priorities among this infinite quantity of goals and models; they are not selective. Although current usage refers to the above-mentioned doctrines as Christian ideology, Marxist ideology, or individualistic ideology, we prefer to reserve the term "ideology" for a different connotation, like for instance the Peking or the Moscow ideology within Marxist doctrine, the reformist or the communitarian revolutionary ideology within Christian social doctrine, the conservative or the progressive ideology within individualistic doctrine.

What is ideology adding to doctrine? What then, is, the specific content of an ideological choice? It appears to be the establishing of priorities among the infinite number of goals proposed by a given doctrine in such a way that any doctrine can give birth to many different ideologies within its own frame. What makes the substance of the ideological choice is the presence of the very concrete hic-et-nunc situation, to which different people or groups, even professing the same doctrinal principles and models, react differently. Their different reactions lead to different sets of priorities, in other words, to different ideologies.

But this is not the end of the story. Once the priority goals have been chosen, there is still place for alternative ways of implementation. The choice of the ways of implementing given priority goals is what we call the choice of policies of development. It clearly appears that there may be many different policies to implement any given ideological choice of priority goals of development. And any policy implies the choice of strategy, implies planning, and implies programming for its implementation.

Any process of development involves, of course, all the unified, logical steps we just defined and distinguished from each other. When discussing Chilean development, we will be focusing mainly on a given set of priority goals which we called communitarian ideology. But, to be more exact, what in this paper will be discussed is what we have defined as a "doctrine."

It must be noted that what we previously said about the role of ideologies is actually, after a more precise definition, the role of what is being defined as a given set of doctrinal models. And if at that stage of the analysis we mentioned collectivism and individualism as ideologies, it was in the current sense of ideology. On the contrary, the articles following in this book, dealing with the ideologies of economic, social, and political development, because discussed at a level closer to the real situation, will unavoidably treat a given set of priorities and will therefore be devoted to examining ideologies of specific aspects of development.

In what immediately follows we will confine ourselves to treating the doctrinal concepts of individualism, collectivism, and personalism.

The other term that has to be defined is overall development, by which we mean an all-inclusive human development, with special emphasis on economic, social, and political development as they will be defined in subsequent articles.

EXTREME SOCIAL DOCTRINES

When the basic problem of the relations between the individual good and the common good is faced, two extreme and partial doctrines have oriented economic, social, and political development. Such are (1) the *individualistic* doctrine based on philosophical liberalism and historically manifested in a capitalist organization of society and (2) the *collectivistic* doctrine based on philosophical Marxism and historically manifested in a communistic organization of society.

The basic assumption of both doctrines is that the common good is identical with the summation of all individual goods. Given this basic identity, says the *individualist*, let us give the individual all opportunities to look after his own interests, his own happiness, his own good, for it is only normal that he will develop his maximum effort and his best capacities if left to himself; and since this is true for all individuals, the result will be the greatest common good of society. Such is the basic reason for the laissez-faire approach to economic, social, and political development.

But, says the *collectivist*, things do not happen that way, because individuals realize that on many occasions they can increase their own good at the expense of somebody else's good, and therefore they will not increase, but probably decrease, the common good. Exploitation of man by man is possible, has actually happened, and has to be stopped. The only possible solution, says the collectivist, is to start the other way around. In view of the basic assumption of the identity between the summation of individual goods and the common good, the best way to secure the maximum good to individuals is to secure directly the common good, and since the responsibility for the common good is the responsibility of social authority, let such authority have all the needed power to do so. Such is the basic reason for the centralized approach to economic, social, and political development.

But, says the individualist, things do not happen that way, because the central authority realizes that in many occasions it can increase the common good at the expenses of some individual's good. Exploitation of man by authority is possible, has actually happened, and has to be stopped.

PERSONALISTIC DOCTRINE

Personalistic doctrine shares the collectivist's criticism of individualistic doctrine, and the individualist's criticism of collectivistic doctrine. Individualistic doctrine stresses efficiency, but it is carried at the expense of equality, and finally, at the expense of efficiency itself. Collectivistic doctrine stresses equality, but it is carried at the expense of efficiency, and finally at the expense of equality itself.

Although there is no "pure" historical example of either individualistic or collectivistic doctrine, those historical experiences
approaching either extreme have suffered such shortcomings,
especially in the field of economic development. The economic
formulae, corresponding to both extreme doctrines, are clear-
cut. Individualists stress private property, free enterprise, and free
markets without limitation. Collectivists stress collective property, public enterprise, and central planning without limitation.

Both extreme doctrines present two basic mistakes: first, the
basic assumption of the identity between the common good
and the summation of all individual goods does not hold true.
Second, both lack concern about mans' need for responsible
participation in the whole process.

Facing such extremes, personalistic doctrine, which is not a
"middle-of-the-way" course, holds, first, that direct attention
has to be given to both, the individual good and the common
good, and, second, that the whole process of social development
has to result from the maximum responsible participation by
all persons involved.

Through concern about the individual's initiative personalistic doctrine secures efficiency, through concern about the common good it secures equality, through concern about people's
responsible participation it enables conflicts between efficiency
and equality, between the common good and the individual
good, to be reduced to a minimum, and people's self-fulfillment
as persons, through free responsibility, to be at a maximum.

The historical test of such doctrine has never existed in
underdeveloped countries. The Chilean experience is the first.

Some of the economic formulae corresponding to such inte-
grative doctrine could be private property with social function,
free communitarian enterprise within planned goals, overall
democratic planning. Some of the social formulae could be the
people's participation through intermediary organizations and
equality of opportunities. Some of the political formulae could
be the subsidiarity principle for the assignment of responsibilities between state and people's organization, and real (as differ-

ent from formal) democracy. But these formulae need further elaboration.

When facing a situation of underdevelopment, the personalistic doctrine, in its search for efficiency, equality, and participation, proposes a change of social structures that has to be rapid, all-inclusive, and deep. In a summary formula, personalistic doctrine, facing Latin American, and Chilean, underdevelopment, rejects any collectivistic-flavored Castro type of revolution and any individualistic-flavored reformist type of development, and endorses any social revolution in freedom.

Part II:
Economic Aspects

3: ECONOMIC ASPECTS OF THE REVOLUTION IN FREEDOM

Ricardo Ffrench-Davis

In the Program of Christian Democracy economic development is to be achieved within a framework of profound social and political reform. Its essence and meaning is a Program for a Revolution in Freedom, some of whose basic economic aspects will here be covered. As these aspects are too numerous to be treated in their totality, I will focus on those that, being, I believe, of more interest to an American reader, are also suitable to show the strong link between the political, economic, and social aspects of the Program.

The Program has a threefold characteristic: it stresses that to achieve economic and social development it must provide equality of opportunities, must promote maximum participation of people in the task, and must create a framework of economic efficiency.

HOW TO JUDGE THE EFFICIENCY OF AN ECONOMIC PROGRAM

To begin with I will center on the role of economic theory. Economic theory is, I believe, of universal validity. In that sense the analytical tools are neutral and nonideological, and ought to be the same everywhere. They are equally applicable to monopoly and perfect competition cases, to price stability and inflation, to growth and to stagnation, to capitalistic, collectivistic, and communitarian systems.

The analytical tools simply constitute the stage of logical

47

analysis. But, when doing economic policy, we meet a prior stage: that of the assumptions. If we want the conclusions of an economic analysis or the effects of economic policy to be those desired, it is necessary that the assumptions we have chosen describe correctly the substance of our economic reality.

What is the importance of this fact for our analysis? Three considerations ought to be mentioned.

First, it is highly important for a correct understanding, in developed countries, of what is happening in the developing world.

In the second place, economic theory has been mainly developed in rich, mature countries, and its exposition and applications deal basically with an economic framework that is that of the developed countries. With frequency, economists trained in the United States and Europe and foreign economic advisers to underdeveloped countries, ignoring the vital role of the kind of framework within which they operate, recommend economic policies that may be sound in their native countries but result in a grand failure in the advised countries. Nevertheless, there is a small but growing legion of economists that are an exception to this rule. I must add that I am aware that in some fields of economic policy the standard recipe is sometimes correct. Hence, in short, the lesson is that an adequate policy in the United States (or Europe) is not *necessarily* always an adequate one in developing countries and, naturally, vice versa.

In the third place, the mixing of valid analytical tools and irrelevant or wrong assumptions is one of the factors that has, unfortunately, led public officials in poor and developing countries to reject and forget about the help that these tools could give. The result is (1) the institution of a highly centralized plan that completely disregards the useful role, in a planning process, of a wisely guided price system and (2) the impulse to industrialization and import substitution patterns that are too far from ideal. In general, industrialization constitutes a wise policy, but what matters is how it is done and what it includes; this procedure cannot be followed with a disregard for the social and economic costs and benefits. In fact, industrialization is not an end in itself. *It is a means to achieve economic development. Some patterns promote economic development; some retard it.*

The approach of the Chilean government, between the two extremes of blind acceptance of textbook recipes and dogmatic rejection of analytical economic tools, has been to make good use of the knowledge of economic theory accumulated through the centuries. But it has taken good care to *readapt* it to the political, economic, and social framework of Chile in order to combine equality of opportunities, people's participation, and efficiency. The efficiency, at last, is to be measured by the degree and speed with which economic, social, and political goals are achieved.

The role of efficiency appears clear when overall development is considered. For example, when full employment, economic growth, elimination of foreign economic and political dependence, development of people's personality, and so on are sought simultaneously, efficiency is crucial. It simply means that the best package of goals is to be achieved with the resources at hand. In this sense efficiency is not morally neutral. The concept of efficiency must imply a permanent respect for human and national dignity. As such, a mean that in some way hurts human rights is, accordingly, an inefficient mean.[1]

After this introduction, let us analyze some of the economic aspects of the Program of the Chilean government: the Program of the Revolution in Freedom.

The Program contains the set of economic, political, and social goals and reforms to be accomplished, the means to achieve them, and the timetable of their execution. These aspects all are so closely related that no policy can be designed without some degree of coordination among them. The Program is ambitious but feasible. Nevertheless, to achieve success

---

[1] An employment policy cannot be satisfied with providing every unemployed worker with a check. It is not the same, for human dignity, to receive a check after performing a proper job as to receive it as an unemployment allowance. An "efficient" employment policy must provide each worker with an opportunity to work.

in all fields there must be a good and, because of its inevitable initial weakness, a *growing* coordination of all policies. Moreover, the persistent failure of some policies can greatly endanger the feasibility of others.

For our purposes the economic aspects can be classified into (1) democratic planning, (2) stabilization of the price level, (3) income redistribution, and (4) economic development.

DEMOCRATIC PLANNING

Economic goals are to be attained within a framework of planning. In this respect there is still much misunderstanding and prejudice about the word "planning." The purpose of planning is simply to influence the facts in such a way that future events conform to our desires. The more underdeveloped an economy, the more planning it needs; the greater the reforms to be instituted, the greater the services planning can lend.[2] But there is good and there is bad planning. To be successful, planning must be deeply realistic and flexible. As a consequence, planning in Chile is to be decentralized in regard to decision-making, that is, to coordinate decisions by centralizing information and making it available to the various economic units, whether private or public, making the decisions.

Let us clarify this a bit with respect to the process of economic decision-making. Different decisions must correspond to different levels. Some are of a macroeconomic and purely technical type, that is, monetary policy, exchange rate policy. Decisions dealing with them must be centralized and made with no intervention by private persons.[3] Others are of a microeconomic character, that is, how best to produce cloth, what

[2] In fact, the more underdeveloped an economy, the higher tends to be the divergence between social and private prices. Planning can be defined as the process that intends to eliminate that divergence.

[3] This is the basic principle behind the proposal to reform the Central Bank. Since its foundation the board of directors of the Central Bank has been controlled by representatives of the private sector.

mix of inputs to use. These decisions must be decentralized, to leave them to the owners of productive agents (labor and/or capital) operating in the enterprises, with no interference (allowing the natural exceptions) of central authorities. There is a third kind of decision which neither the central authorities alone nor the individual enterprises nor citizens can or should make. Who, then, should make those decisions? The answer is the communitarian organizations. In this respect, underdeveloped countries suffer from the absence of these intermediate institutions between the state and the family. This fact leads to extreme individualism, to paternalism, and to the underutilization of people's potentialities. For what people cannot individually do for themselves, they expect the state to provide for, and the state, given its economic limitations, is frequently incapable of so providing. The approach of Christian Democracy consists in filling the vacuum between the state and the family by promoting the formation of communitarian organizations from the local level all the way to the national community.

This strategy leads to development on two fronts: politically, it allows people to have a voice at decision-making centers; economically, it fosters communitarian action in those cases where both individuals and the state are incapable of doing an efficient performance.

In regard to the economic aspect, communitarian organizations should deal with the so-called collective or communitarian goods.[4] For the communitarian organization to be efficient in allocating, financing, and deciding on the production of a collective good, benefits and costs must correspond to this community, not to a bigger or a smaller one. Hence, a collective good of a local character should be dealt by a union of neigh-

---

[4] This is an extension of the old concept of collective goods as appears in economic literature, for example, Richard Musgrave, *The Theory of Public Finance* (New York: McGraw-Hill, 1959). For an analysis in the direction set in here see Joseph Ramos, "Sociedad económica o comunidad de personas ¿una antítesis insuperable?" *Mensaje*, XV, 155 (December 1966). 681–689.

bors. A collective good of a national character should be dealt by a national and social economic committee.

An example appears in the case of a national change in the distribution of daily working hours: such a change not only affects the secular habits of people but also brings about an economic impact concerning the time of greatest utilization of the means of public transportation. A decision of this kind ought to be made at the level of a national (or regional) social and economic committee where intermediate bodies representing all community groups are gathered.

This area of planning is part of *Promoción Popular*, whose purpose is to promote the organization of local, regional, and national communities that would take charge of many of the tasks that at present either rest on the shoulders of the government or are not performed at all. The law giving legal life to this important institution is still waiting for passage by Congress.

STABILIZATION

Chile has suffered from a high rate of inflation for decades. Traditionally, the several efforts to stop inflation have been associated with high unemployment, a fall in output per capita, and a regressive redistribution of income. The purposes of the Chilean government were to stop inflation in a quite different way: to reduce inflation gradually but at the same time to increase output and redistribute income in favor of low-income groups, all within a framework of social and political reform.

Efforts have been successful up to the present in reducing the rate of inflation according to a five-year program set in advance. Nevertheless, there is still a long way to go and hard obstacles to face. The goals will continue to be achieved only if all branches of economic policy are closely coordinated and complemented: in other words, if they are well planned and, second, *if the people play their crucial role.*

When the Christian Democratic government took office in November 1964 the rate of inflation had been 47 percent during the preceding twelve months. The rate was reduced to 26 percent in 1965, to 17 percent in 1966, and efforts are directed to reduce it further in 1967.

At this stage we will discuss only two of the main tools used to eradicate inflation: fiscal policy and foreign trade policy. Other important means have been monetary, price, and wage policies.

1. FISCAL POLICY

The fiscal budget deficit has traditionally been one of the causes of inflation in Chile. Moreover, tax evasion was widespread, and fiscal expenditure concentrated on consumption expenditures rather than on investment. The effort has been sizable in this field, even though, as in every other field, there is much more to be done.

Tax income has increased in two years, 1965 to 1966, by 48 percent in real terms (excluding taxes on copper) as compared with a 13 to 14 percent increase in real gross national product over the same period. The extraordinary increase in fiscal revenue is of a progressive nature as it is due to (a) a strong reduction in tax evasion, (b) the introduction of a tax on wealth that affects people who receive forms of income which are easy to hide and remain undeclared, and who, consequently, evade personal income tax, (c) a transitory tax on banking loans, and (d) a readjustment, in relation to the rate of inflation, of the personal income tax that in Chile is paid after a lag of one year.

If analyzed in detail, it can be found that these reforms all combine equity and efficiency.

Expenditures have also increased but at a somewhat lower rate, and their composition has been improved. While less than 25 percent of fiscal expenditures were devoted to investment in previous periods, more than 36 percent of the increase in expenditures in these last two years has been in investment.

Moreover, the effort to improve the fiscal behavior is reflected in fact that in 1964 only 79 percent of fiscal expenditures were financed with fiscal income, while in 1967 about 91 percent are going to be financed in such a way. In addition, foreign loans accounted for an average of 11 percent of fiscal expenditures from 1961 to 1964. In 1966 this foreign loan percentage was reduced to 9 percent and will be eliminated in 1967 provided the price of copper, the principal export of Chile, remains at its present high level; hence, Chile will make no use of International Monetary Fund and Agency for International Development loans during 1967.

2. EXPORT AND IMPORT POLICY

In Chile the foreign sector is very important. Imports represent about 20 percent of the gross national product. This figure can be contrasted with the low 4 percent of the United States. From this high proportion of imports to the gross national product in Chile there derives the crucial importance of a smooth-working system of importation. As of 1964 the reality was quite far from what is desirable. Let us see why.

Import permits were approved by the Central Bank only after long, uncertain periods of delay. Once permits were approved, no foreign currency was made available to the importer before 120 days after shipment, and the usual situation was that the Central Bank authorized the payment only after six or seven months of delay. Naturally, these facts meant both an increase in real costs for domestic producers who had to keep higher stocks of imported intermediate goods to allow for the uncertainty of having their imports approved, and higher costs charged by foreign suppliers due to the uncertainty of the period in which they were to receive their payment.

Beyond this, exporters and importers were victims of strong uncertainty with respect to the real exchange rate. The exchange rate policy, similar to that of the great part of underdeveloped countries facing inflation, consisted in keeping the exchange rate constant for long periods despite high rates of inflation (even as high as 90 percent per year). Naturally, from time to time the exchange rate had to be devaluated by even 40 or 50 percent. As it can be imagined, after the exchange rate had been fixed for some time and inflation amounted to a significant figure, the foreign currency reserves of Chile tended to disappear, and people connected with financial circles started speculating in dollars in order to reap the capital gains from the devaluation which was likely to come. The loss was borne by the many small Chilean producers of exportable goods who had no way to defend themselves from inflation and from the long period of a pegged exchange rate. This picture was repeated time after time, with the consequent inflationary expectations.

At present, all uncertainty attached to exchange rate policy has been eliminated. The exchange rate is modified continuously, approximately *pari passu* with inflation. In that way no one can profit from speculating in dollars, and exporters and importers know what is going to be the approximate real price of foreign currency. Hence, the most important problems related to the exchange rate and its allocative role have been eliminated.

At the same time, import permits are licensed immediately and payments made promptly. In that way the foreign trade of Chile is normalized, and no significant uncertainties are derived from the economic policy followed. The high returns of this efficient and sound policy are appreciated by comparing the increase, during the period 1965 to 1966, of 50 percent in the exchange rate[5] versus an increase of only about 25 percent in the price of imported goods on Chilean markets. Part of the

---

[5] In the same period, the twenty-six months running from November 1964 to December 1966, consumer prices rose in Chile 46 percent over their increase in the United States. In such a way, the real exchange rate rose by almost 4 percent. At the same time the terms of trade showed a strong improvement for Chile. For additional information see *Boletín Mensual*, Banco Central de Chile.

difference represented the effect of uncertainty due to exchange-rate policy on the cost of imported goods.

The third important aspect, with respect to the external sector, refers to the tariff structure. This has not been essentially modified, although several marginal improvements have been made. It has been recognized in several documents before and after the current administration took office that its present structure hides serious distortions. The fundamental modification of the tariff structure constitutes a future step to be made in order that the external sector of Chile serves more effectively as a road to economic development.

INCOME REDISTRIBUTION

In order to redistribute income several measures were taken: some of a short-run nature, purely redistributive; others of a long-run nature and of a type where equity and economic efficiency move together.

1. WAGE SYSTEM

In an economy that has suffered inflation for a long period it is quite probable that the wage system is grossly distorted. This happened for example in the public administration and in the countryside: in different sectors people of the same ability who were performing the same work were earning different salaries and wages. Wage policy has been directed toward correcting those distortions and injustices. The full correction takes time and, in some cases, they are to be done gradually in periods of three or four years. By the same token, real minimum wages have been increased up to the point where the structure of the economy allowed, without deriving in undesired unemployment.

2. FAMILY ALLOWANCES

These differed widely among different labor categories. The Christian Democratic government has been progressively equal-izing them by applying the idea that all Chilean children, no matter what their economic origin, deserve exactly the same family allowance. Otherwise the family allowances, instead of giving equal opportunities to all children, discriminate against children whose parents belong to non-unionized and blue-collar employee groups.

3. EDUCATION

The provision of education for all Chilean children and at the same time the improvement in the quality of education is the overwhelmingly basic long-run tool of income redistribution.

The year 1965 was devoted to permitting every child to be admitted to the first year of primary school. (In 1965 primary education comprised six years; in 1967 it covered eight years.) The year 1966 was devoted to permitting all children leaving the sixth year of primary school to enter the next stage. At this step there was a serious shortage of facilities in the educational system that forced the dropout of many students.

The results of this determined quantitative effort have been an increase of 13 percent, 30 percent, and 12 percent of the number of students in the primary, secondary, and professional branches of education, respectively. Simultaneously, there have been broad training courses for new and old teachers, and summer courses for students in the field of education in order to accelerate their training.

School buildings are being used more intensively. At the same time the government has almost doubled its annual investment in the building of new schools. At this point it is important to mention the contribution of the community to the educational program. There are countless cases of labor unions that (with no tax incentives) have financed school buildings out of the pockets of their own members. Likewise, community organizations of low-income counties have organized to finance and build by themselves school buildings for their children.

But, also, side by side the efforts of the communities mentioned above must be mentioned the truly generous contribution of the university students. By the hundreds they have been devoting their summer vacations to serving the community. Student unions have organized their members and moved to the poorest regions of the country during the summer months. There they have undertaken a variety of tasks according to their training: assisting people in building schools and houses, dispensing medical and dental services, organizing cooperatives, and giving short courses on different disciplines useful to the people. The only motive pushing these students has been the purpose to contribute to build a new and better society.

Lastly, the training of workers to keep pace with technical innovations is being broadly extended. Nevertheless, it is not enough to build classrooms and form teachers. It is also necessary to attack the dropout of students due to economic reasons. Besides the other direct ways of redistributing income, scholarships, loans, free lunches, and breakfasts have been either introduced or vastly extended in order to retain the potentially abler pupil.

As it can be seen, once again we find efforts to bring together equal opportunities, efficiency, and people's participation.

4. Agrarian Reform

The agrarian reform is, in my judgment, primarily a social reform. But it also serves an economic purpose as it puts to work idle lands and develops fully the productive capacity of the peasants by giving them better opportunities and greater responsibilities. Everywhere agrarian reforms have been frequently characterized by anarchy and a drop in production during their transition period. Because of its design, the process in Chile is to be generally orderly and organized. There is a transition period of two to three years in which the Agrarian Reform Corporation (CORA) assists directly the peasants in technical aspects and in which productive practices are only gradually changed. Moreover, all efforts are directed to prepare people, in organized communities, to be able to make good decisions on their own in the future and to participate in a responsible way in shaping their future destiny.

In the end the agrarian reform will mean a change of the previously existing feudal power structure into a democratic power structure in the countryside, an efficient contribution to economic development, and a permanent redistribution of wealth and income. In this process the mere redistribution of land is not in itself a sufficient factor.

5. TAX SYSTEM

Finally, we can again mention briefly the redistributive role of the tax system, which has been gradually modified toward serving both the roles of redistributing income and of financing fiscal expenditures (much of which are also directed toward income redistribution, that is, school breakfasts and lunches).

ECONOMIC DEVELOPMENT

The rate of increase of the gross national product (GNP), the best available measure of economic development, has greatly accelerated in Chile. In the last two years the annual growth has been above 6 percent while in the last two decades the rate of growth was about 3.5 percent.[6]

What could be called an extraordinary improvement of the rate of growth has resulted from a better and more efficient use of existing resources. For example, industrial output has risen 10 percent per year. Of this increase, more than half corresponds to better utilization of the productive capacity already installed as of 1964. The improvement of efficiency is the programmed result of the set of economic policies directed to that end: reduction of inflation, correction of distortions in the price system, normalization of the supply of foreign raw materials

[6] In per-capita figures the rate has been increased from 1 percent to 4 percent.

and repair parts, improvement in the distribution of credit, and so on. Nevertheless, improvements in efficiency bring about only one-time increases in output. Consequently, for further increases in output, efficiency must be maintained at a high level, and, over and above this, the availability of resources must increase. Here we meet the importance of the capitalization of the economy and its level of savings. Savings have been extraordinarily low in Chile in past decades, the average figure having been about 10 percent of GNP. To be able to sustain, after efficiency improvements have done their part, a rate of growth of 6 to 7 percent, savings must reach a figure of approximately 20 percent of GNP (in order to finance the required investments in education, social and physical capital). The task is a gigantic one, and we are only at the beginning of the journey. To face it, two kinds of measures should be at hand. One is to keep savings from losing their purchasing power as long as inflation continues. In this regard, saving instruments that are readjustable according to inflation have been either created or extended.[7] But, in my judgment, further complementary policies are needed if the task is to double gross savings and foster a rapid process of redistribution. At this stage we can introduce an analogy. During World War II citizens of the United States were filled with such a spirit that they were fully willing to incur sacrifices. One of them was to postpone present consumption. Chile is also experiencing a war, a war against economic and social backwardness in favor of eradicating inflation, poverty, injustice, and dependence on foreign assistance.

It is the task of the government to create an atmosphere that makes every Chilean feel this war of economic and social development is his own. People should manifest their feeling in their savings behavior, in their participation in community organizations, and as members of the labor force. The essence of the

---

[7] The present main source of personal savings, time deposits at the State Bank, have been made readjustable. They comprise .8 million accounts of medium- and low-income people, as compared to a labor force of some 3 million workers and a population of 8.5 million inhabitants.

process is not only that the reforms and efforts are all directed to favor the people. A necessary condition is that all people clearly recognize that fact: that it is, at last, their government. This condition is fulfilled when people are conscious that the success of the overall development enterprise depends vitally on their full participation. The recipe to create this atmosphere[8] should vary from place to place, and this is the aspect of the Program where divergence between effective results and programmed results are more noticeable.

I want to end my exposition by dealing with one field within economic development where the role of assumptions once again explains the widely differing policies that developed and underdeveloped countries *should* follow.

One of the instruments on which Latin American countries count to promote their economic development is the integration of their domestic markets into one Latin American common market. Such a market promotes economic development by allowing industrialization to continue along with the benefits accruing from economies of scale and economic specialization. For countries with any degree of development a common market leads to a further economic specialization allowing the utilization at full capacity of industries with economies of scale. But the differences appear when the precise structure of the institutions created to move toward a common market is designed. If the integrating markets do have widely differing degrees of development, the great bulk of new industries will be attracted to the more developed markets. In fact, these already can count on more developed financial institutions, trained and more efficient labor, complementary industries, and better means of transportation.

The six member countries of the European Common Market had similar industrial levels. In Latin America the degrees of development differ greatly from country to country. Conse-

[8] See J. Ahumada, *La crisis integral de Chile* (Santiago de Chile: Editorial Universitaria, 1966), esp. pp. 39–44.

quently, if no consideration is taken of this fact, a Latin American common market of the European type would lead to a concentration of all benefits in those countries that are already stronger. Hence, in the case of Latin America, institutions should be designed to solve a danger that in the case of Europe did not exist. The corresponding changes to the Chilean Constitution proposed by the government and the suggestions of Chile to improve the Charter of the Latin American Free Trade Association go somewhat in that direction.

For the less-developed countries within Latin America the existence or nonexistence of those institutions will determine whether they benefit or suffer from economic integration.

In summary, the analytical tools at hand are in both cases the same, but the assumptions that describe the economic reality differ from place to place. To judge the efficiency of an economic and social program, the assumptions of the judge—foreign or domestic economic adviser or politician—must describe correctly the reality of the judged country.

To be able to perform a radical change in the economic and social structure of an underdeveloped country and be successful, a clear knowledge of the economic, political, and social reality must be at hand. Political parties and leaders that do well understand their environment and succeed in incorporating all people in the process of change and development ought to be successful in their efforts of changing their society into a better one.

That is the way chosen by the Chilean Revolution in Freedom. It is a long way, with successes and failures, but it leads to the right place.

4: THE ECONOMIC DEVELOPMENT
OF CHILE: PAST AND PRESENT
Tom E. Davis

INTRODUCTION AND CONCLUSIONS

Chile was considered, prior to independence, to be one of the more impoverished components of the Spanish colonial empire. In contrast, at the time of the Great Depression Chile stood with Argentina and Uruguay as among the most prosperous nations in Latin America. By implication, the republic's first century was characterized by rapid economic progress. Against this backdrop the post-Depression period, particularly the years following the end of the Korean War, appears as an era of relative economic retardation.

The historical perspective suggests that the failure of Chile to effect a successful transition from the export-oriented economy of the nineteenth century to a modern industrial technocracy of the twentieth century is due to the fact that (1) economic change during the nineteenth century failed to produce a basic alteration in the political and social structure, and (2) external events (World War I and the Great Depression) precipitated economic and political changes in the twentieth century that resulted in a nonfunctional economy and the dominance of the urban middle class. Currently, adoption of a set of economic policies that would increase the efficiency of the economy is limited by constraints imposed by the existing political structure. Long retarded social change, which will incorporate the rural proletariat into the polity as an autonomous political group, is a prerequisite for breaking the immobil-

izing political dominance of the urban middle class and for the
emergence of rational economic decision-making and increased
productivity throughout the economy. Christian Democracy
appeals to pervasive humanist values to induce the now dominant political groups to accept programs that will accelerate
social change and increase economic efficiency at the expense
of short-run individual economic self-interest. By supporting
land redistribution the Christian Democrats also are appealing
to the rural proletariat in attempting to broaden their political
base and ultimately to reduce their dependence upon the urban
middle class.

POLITICAL AND SOCIAL RETARDATION IN THE
CONTEXT OF NINETEENTH-CENTURY
ECONOMIC EXPANSION

Sustained economic growth in Chile began shortly after Diègo
Portales, the first and least repressive of Latin America's "unify-
ing dictators," ushered in an era of stability and legality shortly
after the republic was established "by reason or by force." Thus,
Chile was the first of the new nations to satisfy Adam Smith's
elemental conditions for augmenting national wealth. In the
1840's Chilean grain on Chilean bottoms fed Limeños, gold
prospectors in California, and immigrants in Australia. Chilean
bonds sold near par in London, while Argentine securities could
be purchased at substantial discounts.

Despite the promising beginning, successive Chilean governments did not always succeed in channeling foreign capital into
the development of railways and port facilities, thus to reduce
the cost of exports and add to the nonagricultural demand for
labor services. As the century drew to a close, governments
increasingly borrowed abroad in order to purchase mortgages
from landowners, only a part of which was invested in clearing
additional acreage, pulling up fencing, and constructing dams
and irrigating canals. The real value of this peso debt declined
as prices rose steadily after 1879, fueled by government deficits

generated initially to finance the war against Bolivia and Peru, but sustained subsequently to continue the earlier policy of extending credit to now politically dominant agricultural interests at negative real rates of interest. The precedent for the utilization of the public powers to serve the short-run economic interests of the dominant members of the polity at the expense of the provision of the basic political and social infrastructure was established at a time when Chile's economic position was most promising and would have permitted a simultaneous expansion both of investment and consumption.

Following the War of the Pacific, the legitimacy of the Chilean government was further compromised by an event that placed a permanent stigma on foreign ownership and control. The war had its origins in the dispute between Chilean operators of nitrate properties in the Atacama Desert and the governments of Bolivia and Peru that claimed their rights to the subsoil as successors to the Hapsburgs and Bourbons. When the Bolivian and Peruvian governments issued certificates of ownership to these "Chilean" mines, the Chilean government, ostensibly at least, mobilized to protest Chilean property rights. To the astonishment of all, the Chilean Congress declared valid the certificates of ownership issued by their defeated adversaries. Surprise gave way to cynicism when one John North, an Englishman who had been active in the area and apparently in the Chilean Congress, revealed that he had acquired the bulk of these certificates and therefore controlled the nitrate industry. Chilean entrepreneurship in the mining industry had little chance to develop.

These nitrate properties enhanced in value enormously as the nineteenth century drew to a close. Effectively taxed by the Chilean government, nitrates represented a source of finance for social, as well as physical, infrastructure. Liberal President José Balmaceda presented a program that promised a more fundamental restructuring of the economy and society than the Conservatives were prepared to accept. The elitist navy defeated Balmaceda's army in a civil war, and the President committed suicide. The resistance of the landowner-capitalist to accept a popular government that would promote economic opportunity and social justice was manifest long before governments imposed export quotas and domestic price ceilings on agricultural products. By World War I Chile's noted historian Francisco Encina had discerned "our economic inferiority" and attributed it to the failure of government to provide universal basic education. Nearly a century of sustained growth had failed to result in the incorporation of the bulk of the rural population into the market economy or into autonomous political parties.

EXOGENOUSLY ACCELERATED ECONOMIC AND POLITICAL CHANGE IN THE TWENTIETH CENTURY

Then World War I rocked the foundations of Chile's economy. Europe's iron and steel industry grew, and in Germany a process was developed to convert its gaseous by-product, previously industrial waste, into synthetic (ammonium) nitrate fertilizer. Despite the resulting loss of the bulk of the European fertilizer market, Chile gained some respite when foreign entrepreneurship and capital proceeded to develop the copper industry.[1] The center of international lending shifted from London to New York, within the consequence that in 1925 the Kemmerer Mission designed the new Chilean Central Bank along the lines of the Federal Reserve System rather than the Bank of England. General Carlos Ibáñez, however, proved to be as adept in persuading New York financiers to extend credits as his more conservative predecessors had been in London. Foreign loans along with nitrate and copper revenues were parlayed into a financial base that permitted the bureaucracy to expand sufficiently to satisfy the aspirations of the urban middle class that had gained political ascendancy in 1920 with the election of

[1] Alas, the Guggenheim interests—better known in the academic community for the benefices provided to itinerant scholars—sold the Chuquicamata copper properties to Anaconda and invested the proceeds in nitrate properties whose value in relation to the copper properties fell markedly over the time.

Arturo Alessandri. Simultaneously, Chile, together with Argentina and Uruguay, led Latin America in the development of social security and labor legislation whose "coverage" admittedly was limited largely to white-collar employees. Even these measures, however, did not suffice to save the Ibáñez government when the Great Depression eliminated foreign borrowing and greatly curtailed export revenues, but they did moderate the radicalism of the period.

The urban middle class proceeded to defend their short-run economic interests within the constraints imposed by foreign exchange availabilities. Imports no longer could satisfy the growing urban market for manufactured goods. Effective demand was sustained when the government was compelled by political exigencies to revert to the traditional practice of sustaining public expenditures by borrowing from the banking system, which in turn printed money to cover the deficits produced by the reduction in revenues obtained from taxes on exports and imports.

Regardless of the policy adopted to tailor the demand for foreign exchange to fit the greatly reduced supply, domestic firms, many of which had commenced operations when imports had been curtailed during World War I, would have expanded production. The Chileans chose quotas in preference to tariffs or an increase in the price of foreign exchange.[2] The largest allocations were reserved for fuels, industrial raw materials, and capital goods at the expense of final products. The "induced industrialization" that occurred in the thirties was attributed, ex post facto, to the "import substitution policy."

A labor force was hastily recruited by "novice" industrialists whose success was assured because potential competitors were unlikely to obtain the foreign exchange to set up rival plants as long as demand for other "import substitutes" remained unsatisfied. Labor productivity appeared low, and plant routines

[2] Prior to World War II cartel arrangements in the copper industry would have negated any stimulus to exports that a higher price for foreign exchange might have provided in a competitive world market.

remained frozen. The domestic market was limited to the urban half of a population of 7 million (1952) and economies of scale in manufacturing dictated that a few firms would dominate most industries even when imported capital goods were readily available. Many of these firms could pass on to the consumer at least a part of the social security "tax" that progressively rose to the point where it constituted as much as 50 percent of money wages; large firms in industries like food processing, textiles, clothing, and wood and leather products had to compete with small "workshops" that evaded their obligations and consequently absorbed most, if not all, of the "tax."

ECONOMIC RETARDATION

The market was protected from foreign competition, but it was not growing. The export sector no longer expanded employment or provided the revenues to the government to finance expansion of the public sector employment. After World War II, employment in the large firms in the dominant copper industry actually fell by one-half because successive governments retained the 19.26 peso (= U.S.$1) exchange rate during the interval from the Great Depression to 1955. During this period the domestic price level rose approximately 20 percent per annum and wage rates in the copper industry increased even more rapidly. The price of capital goods fell markedly in relation to the price of labor, which with the constant 19.26 exchange rate was increasing in terms of dollars at the same rate that peso wage costs were rising. As a consequence the copper industry imported the most labor-saving equipment; capital for expansion of facilities was directed toward Peru, Rhodesia, and even marginal mines in the United States.

These same governments did not sell the foreign exchange, purchased from the copper companies at the 19.26 rate, at the maximum the traffic would bear (and by 1955 the price of a United States dollar in the "free," or black, market had reached

800 pesos), but rather made this foreign exchange available for the importation of certain classes of "necessities" at a range of prices (or preferential exchange rates) that produced little revenue for the government. The beneficiaries were the consumers of these imported products (typically the urban middle class) if their prices were controlled effectively or the importers if the controls were ineffective. In either case, however, the employment generated was minimal as compared to what might have been produced if the government had maximized its receipts and used the proceeds to pay wages and salaries.

Chilean agricultural exports received substantially better treatment than did copper, but the country passed from the status of "net exporter" to that of "net importer" of agricultural products, as agricultural production rose at approximately the same rate as population increased. Whether the relative prices of agricultural products has risen in Chile since the Great Depression has been the source of considerable debate. In any event, cultivated acreage never surpassed the levels attained prior to the Great Depression, and the slow rate of increase in money incomes generated in agriculture provided little stimulus to the manufacturing sector.

As a result, employment in manufacturing failed to expand after 1952. Prior to that time manufacturing had constituted the dynamic sector of the Chilean economy. Limited not only by a small and relatively stagnant domestic market but also by static production routines and, hence, rising unit labor costs (resulting from the elaboration of the labor and social security legislation), Chile's manufactured products had little success in world markets. It is not surprising that since the end of the Korean War the service sector of the Chilean economy has expanded relatively in relation to the other sectors, and the rate of inflation accelerated.[3]

---

[3] The "tip-off" that all was not well with the manufacturing sector was provided by the 1948 law that provided for limitations on capital goods imports into Chile. Confronted by a stagnant tax-base, the government had little political alternative to printing money to expand employment in the public sector.

CONTEMPORARY ECONOMIC PROBLEMS

What insight can be gained from this historical perspective of the evolution of the Chilean economy? A picture emerges of an economy with successive sectors providing dynamism for a limited time only, thus to stagnate subsequently. In the mid-nineteenth century Chile expanded its agricultural frontiers and exported agricultural products; a succession of liberal and conservative governments borrowed abroad and purchased mortgages from agricultural landowners who invested in irrigation facilities. After the War of the Pacific the "encouragement" of foreign investment resulted in the expansion of nitrate exports. Nitrates are replaced by copper in relative importance in the late 1920's, and copper production expanded to World War II. The Great Depression stimulates the growth of manufacturing, which persisted to the end of the Korean War.

Preferential treatment thus appears to be required to stimulate sectorial growth in Chile. Agriculture expanded when capital was available at essentially negative rates of interest after 1879. Nitrate exports developed when governments were prepared to alienate territory only recently annexed by virtue of victory in a costly war, to devalue repeatedly, and to limit taxation on nitrate exports. Finally, industry required the protection from foreign competition that emerged as a result of the permanent implantation of the system of quotas developed to adjust to the fall of foreign exchange receipts that occurred during the Great Depression.

By definition, government cannot provide privileged treatment to all sectors simultaneously. The encouragement of industry has clearly taken place at the expense of the copper and agricultural exports and deteriorating terms-of-trade for the agricultural sector. The size of the market for industrial products has been limited by the consequent loss of dynamism in the export sector and virtual stagnation in the agricultural sector.

Effective market size can be expanded by increasing the efficiency of productivity of the domestic economy. A modern economy is characterized by increases in productivity of 1 to 3 percent per annum over sustained periods of time. Furthermore, only 20 to 25 percent of economic growth in the United States is attributed to additions to the capital stock. The remainder is forthcoming from increasing the productivity of existing plants and equipment, unassociated with substantial amounts of capital investment. It comes essentially from new methods of organization of plants, of small adjustments that greatly enhance the efficiencies of existing equipment—things that are very difficult to identify and that frequently in econometric analyses are put into a residual category.

One explanation for the failure of productivity to increase in Chilean industry stems from the fact that it is manned basically by a first-generation labor force, recruited during a relatively short period of time from a traditional, if not in all instances, rural population. The confrontation with the urban environment may very well produce a value orientation in a second generation that will increase motivation and the flexibility of routines in industrial establishments.

The stagnation in agriculture is frequently attributed to this same loss of the mobile elements in the rural labor. The argument is analogous to the old "saw" about the professor who leaves Podunk College for State University and lowers the average in both institutions. The fact remains that the maximum of cultivated agricultural acreage was reached in 1930. Since that date, when the provision of irrigation of acreage became a prerogative of the state, public investment has been directed toward the urban areas (especially toward power and transportation), and few resources have been channeled into irrigation facilities. The land tenure structure in agriculture and the limited participation of agricultural labor in politics contributed to the "pariah" treatment that agriculture has received and the lack of entrepreneurship due (at least in part) to the extreme rigidity of the social structure has insured a defensive, contractionist response.

The inability of Chile to confront its economic problems produced by this lack of dynamism (for example, to curtail the rate of inflation, increase public revenues, introduce a truly comprehensive social security system, raise the real price of foreign exchange and public services) is due to the political structure. Urban middle-class political groups have printed money to defray the cost of expanding white-collar employment in the public sector, refused to increase taxation, insisted upon preferential benefits for white-collar employees, and refused to pay more for social benefits, food, public utility services, or imported commodities. The challenge to these groups can only come from the incorporation into the body politic of the rural proletariat in autonomous political groups. This incorporation failed to occur because external events (World War I and the Great Depression) transferred political power to the urban middle class before export-oriented economic expansion could incorporate the rural population into the labor market. The growth of the industrial sector ceased before it could make a significant impact on the wage rate in rural areas.

THE ROLE OF CHRISTIAN DEMOCRACY IN CHILE

If there is to be true cooperation in the enterprise, be it industrial or agrarian, public or private, common values must override disparate individual values and resolve what otherwise is a conflict situation with attendant low (or falling) productivity. The general, or national, good must be appealed to as a rationale for economic policies that will maximize economic efficiency. It is the function of ideology to provide such justification and to sketch in the relationship between individual behavior and the achievement of the indicated goals.

Christian Democracy in Chile has attempted to provide this new ideology, based upon the "social encyclicals." In terms of program, an attempt has been made (1) to enforce the existing tax legislation, (2) to extend the coverage and reduce the degree of discrimination in the social security and minimum wage system, (3) to increase the degree of Chilean ownership control in the copper industry as a prelude to increasing the real price of foreign exchange, and (4) to embark on a land-reform program to more equitably distribute power, income, and wealth in the rural areas.

The Christian Democratic party is attempting to recruit the rural proletariat by promising to use the power of the government to stimulate the social change that economic expansion failed to induce. If successful, it will reduce its dependence upon the urban middle class and facilitate the solution of contemporary economic problems. In addition, basic social change may prove to be the condition for permitting productivity to increase pervasively throughout the economy, thus to end the pattern of single-sector growth (in response to preferential treatment) that has tended to characterize the evolution of the Chilean economy.

5: SPECIFIC PROBLEMS IN THE ECONOMIC DEVELOPMENT OF CHILE

Arnold Harberger

The scope of this topic is such that I will have to touch lightly upon many subjects, and at the same time I will certainly leave some important problems untouched. This is unfortunate. Yet for clarity I have chosen to organize this presentation under five main headings: the development policy problems that emerge as we study, in turn, the labor market, the product markets, the capital market, and foreign exchange market, and the problems of inflation and stabilization policy in Chile.

Let me turn first to the labor market. All observers agree that the Chilean labor market is characterized by widespread differences in wages received. In many areas of the countryside there is a genuine and direct exploitation of labor in which advantage is taken of the ignorance of Chilean *compesinos* of the alternatives available to them in other parts of the Chilean economy, and in which intimidation and threats are also present at times. At the same time, and at the other end of the spectrum, there are a few distinctly privileged groups in the Chilean labor market. These groups earn wages which are substantially above the average market rate. They in part are located in the large foreign-owned mining companies, which as a matter of policy pay wages far above the market; and they are also present to some degree in certain industries where union power is especially strong.

Minimum wage legislation can help to combat the outright exploitation of the Chilean peasant, but it cannot by itself create a greater or a stronger market for labor than would exist in the absence of exploitation. A minimum wage that is above the market level will lead employers to hire less labor and will thus either generate unemployment or lead to a transfer of labor to sectors of the economy not covered by the minimum-wage legislation, thus to depress the level of wages in these non-covered sectors. Excessively high minimum wages in the manufacturing sector, for example, while surely improving the lot of workers employed in manufacturing, also tend to reduce employment in manufacturing and depress wages in agriculture, services, and other areas. It is thus doubtful whether the average wage of the entire labor force is increased by having high minimum wages in specific sectors. Likewise, an excessively high minimum real wage covering the whole labor force would result in widespread unemployment.

I believe that the hidden exploitation of labor is much more important in Chile than direct exploitation. The failure to provide education and to develop the latent capacities of the youth leaves them inevitably behind—inevitably in a servile role vis-à-vis the more educated. As a society achieves truly general education, somebody must still occupy the bottom rungs of the employment ladder, but in a well-developed and well-educated society the people who occupy the bottom rungs are more productive, are better remunerated, and have more human dignity than is, for example, the case in Chile today. Quite serious, too, in Chile is the problem of upward social mobility. I believe it is perfectly fair to say that no society in the Americas has been more receptive to European immigration than has the Chilean. Many immigrants of the 1930's and the 1940's are today members of Chile's high society, belong to important clubs, and are among the directors and managers of the largest companies and banks. Yet while the upper reaches of Chilean society have, so to speak, accepted with open arms the immigrants who came to Chile from Europe, they have not treated in the same way Chileans who are not themselves born into the upper and upper-middle classes.

I am sure that the educational barrier is the most serious here, but I also suspect that there have been more subtle barriers—barriers based on a defensive, class-oriented psychology—which have operated to keep the children of the poor from rising. This attitude is reflected in the fact that Chilean farmers have not been quick to put their farms into the hands of trained managers (in which case they would have been forced to accept their managers as more or less social equals), but they have instead largely operated in the traditional way by using a trusted *inquilino* as foreman (against whom they maintain a distinct class separation). This is so even though their farms are surely less productive with an *inquilino* foreman than with a trained manager. Similarly, it is my strong impression that, at least in comparison with the United States, family enterprises are much more family oriented: it is family members rather than the most qualified persons who in Chile tend to get the lion's share of the responsible and decision-making jobs.

I feel that the ideological force of the Christian Democratic Program is an important element in breaking down these traditional types of indirect exploitation. Although it must be admitted that prior governments have substantially developed the educational system—indeed, improved education has been one of the major sources of Chile's economic growth in the past—it remains true that the present government is doing much better on this front. It is to be hoped that as the national conscience becomes stronger in these respects, and as more and more people are brought to see the fundamental justice of equal opportunity for all and equal treatment of equals, the doors of upward social mobility will open wider to provide a fulfilling outlet for energies previously contained and at the same time to contribute to the economic growth of the country.

I am especially pleased with the concentration of the Chilean government on breaking specific barriers to education. Setting the goal of universal attendance by first-grade students in 1965, and tackling the goal of a greatly enlarged continuation from the last year of primary school to the first year of secondary school in 1966, represents intelligent planning and a dramatic commitment in the educational field. The consequences of this commitment will be felt for many years to come. In 1966, for example, there were two years of almost-universal primary education; by 1967 this will be three years; in 1968, four years; and so on. The budgetary implication of this year-by-year expansion of the Chilean educational system to accommodate more and more enlarged cohorts are very powerful indeed, and they reflect the depth of Chile's commitment to its goal of social improvement through more and better education.

Let me now turn to the problems arising in the markets for final products in Chile. One of the pervasive aspects of Chilean economic development over the past three decades has been the process of import substitution based on a high degree of protection. Much of this process has been essentially willy-nilly: a foreign exchange crisis occurs and leads to the exclusion of luxury products which then are produced internally at high cost, and soon an industry becomes entrenched. The objective, for example, was not to develop a refrigerator industry for its own sake, but rather to use scarce foreign exchange for purposes more important than importing refrigerators. The consequence —as distinct from the purpose—was the establishment of a high-cost refrigerator industry in Chile.

Although part of the import-substitution process was, in the sense indicated above, not a conscious policy of guiding the course of Chilean industrialization, another part of the process has been conscious. The recent moves in Chile to establish a local automobile industry have been of this type. The government has in this case consciously sponsored the development of a tremendously high-cost industry. A study by Leland Johnson of automobile costs in Chile showed that the costs of saving a dollar of foreign exchange by producing automobiles at home amounted in 1964 to about five times the price of the dollar. Here we must ask why. Also, I must ask why the Chilean government (and many other governments as well) have been so reluctant to take advantage of one of the world's greatest bargains—the used-car market in the United States. A six-year-old American car, worth something like four hundred dollars in the United States market, carries a price tag of three thousand dollars or more in the Chilean market. The possibility of the Chilean government arranging for the importation of used cars is a real and attractive one, and would require a minimal amount of foreign exchange. I am personally confident that this is indeed the most economic way for Chile to meet its needs for motor-vehicle passenger transportation.

A second problem in the product-market area is competition. In point of fact, the degree of monopoly in Chilean industry is many times that prevailing in the United States or in Western Europe. And, viewed in a certain light, monopoly seems almost necessary for Chile in many industries. For, with a gross national product of about 4 billion dollars and a population of 8 to 9 million people, the internal market is simply not large enough to justify more than one or two plants producing a product in which the minimum economic scale is high. If left to themselves in this situation, firms will have a strong incentive to charge high monopolistic prices and exploit their monopoly power at the expense of consumers. They will also not be pressed by competitive forces to improve their products and lower their costs in the same way as occurs naturally in countries with much larger markets. The answer here is, in my view, not an attempt to regulate in detail the pricing and production policies of Chilean enterprises, but rather to subject them to genuine competition. And if competition cannot be generated internally, which is the case for many industries, then that competition must necessarily come from abroad.

This brings me to the problem of the Latin American Free Trade Association (LAFTA). While many kind and hopeful words about LAFTA are expressed by leaders of many parties everywhere in Latin America, the fact remains that to date LAFTA has achieved little, if anything, along the lines of generating effective international competition among the Latin

American countries. No Latin American country appears to be willing to subject its industry to the threat of lower-cost competition, even if that competition comes from its LAFTA partners. Yet it must be emphasized that the true advantages of a free-trade area or a common market really stem from the brisk and vigorous competition among alternative sources of supply which a large market area permits. The LAFTA countries have not yet revealed themselves willing to take those steps which would permit their achieving the principal benefits which LAFTA could potentially bring to them.

Similar comments can be made concerning competition from outside of LAFTA. Industry, once established in Chile, seems to have almost unlimited access to government support to protect it against threatened competition from abroad. How much more should Chile be prepared to pay for something made at home than for the same thing made abroad? There are several reasons by which some differential—some premium for home products as against imported products—may be justified. But these reasons are not forceful enough to justify the payment of 50 percent or 100 percent more for domestic as against imported products. Yet, in Chile the prices of many home-produced items are much more than 50 or 100 percent more costly than their imported counterparts. This is especially true when account is taken of the fact that many manufactured products made in Chile use substantial quantities of imported components, so that the dollar-savings involved in their production at home is only a fraction of the price that they would have to pay for importing the final product. These problems—of rationalizing the industrial structure of Chile and of achieving effective and vigorous competition for domestic enterprises— have been badly mishandled by previous governments in Chile and have simply not yet been confronted by the present one.

Then there are the problems connected with the capital market in Chile. In technical terms these problems have been a lack of an adequate incentive to save and a lack of institutions for appropriately distributing capital throughout the economy. This condition has its main roots in the inflationary process which Chile has suffered and in the way in which Chile has adapted to this inflationary process in the past. In brief, savers in Chile who held money in the form of cash or who placed it in bank deposits have perennially suffered real losses as the purchasing power of their savings was eroded by inflation. By the same token borrowers in Chile have enjoyed real gains, as inflation made their debts become less and less burdensome. This has led (1) to an inefficient distribution of investable funds in society, (2) to an absolute drying up of medium- and long-term credit through the banking system, and (3) to a reduction in the national savings rate below what it might otherwise have been.

With respect to (1), one must realize that everybody in Chile would like to have bank loans in a situation in which what is repaid represents only 75 or 80 percent of the real purchasing power of what was borrowed. Under these circumstances the central bank simply had to limit bank loans, for otherwise the demand would be virtually infinite. This indeed they did, but not by raising the effective price of credit so as to limit demand. The result was that loans were rationed out by the bank—principally into traditional channels but also to friends and maybe relatives of the bankers. Many worthy projects in Chile have remained unfinanced over the years while less productive projects were financed through this inefficient system of allocating the available credit.

With respect to (2), banks in Chile have traditionally refused to lend for medium- and long-term periods a currency threatened with continual deterioration of purchasing power. It may be objected that the banks would lose an equal amount through deterioration of purchasing power by lending for, say, two years as by lending a sequence of eight loans for periods of three months each. There is some merit in this objection, but the institutional arrangements with regard to interest rates has been such in Chile that banks have had good reason to believe that if the pace of inflation increases, interest rates will rise somewhat in the future. Hence, by making short commitments the banks maintain the flexibility to take advantage of any increase in interest rates which may be allowed. In any event, the fact remains that medium- and long-term credit has been sorely lacking in the Chilean economy. Some longer-term loans have been granted by the Chilean Development Corporation (CORFO), but these loans were generally on excessively generous terms, and the borrowers benefited enormously by the credits thus obtained.

In general, those in Chile who were lucky enough to receive credit obtained an effective gift of a large component of that credit, and those who were unlucky received no credit at all, regardless of how meritorious a use they could have made of it.

With respect to (3), the impact of inflation on savings rates has come because of the fact that the interest paid on deposits was typically far below the loss of purchasing power to the depositor. There is no necessity for this to happen because there are ways of protecting savings against inflation.

Gradually, over the past eight years or so, institutions have developed in Chile which tend to protect the saver. During the early years of Alessandri's regime substantial government support was given to a system in which savers could make deposits in the form of dollars. Simultaneously the government issued bonds denominated in terms of dollars. To the extent that the exchange rate moves to reflect the purchasing power of currency, a dollar deposit or a dollar bond is protected against inflation. In point of fact, during the Alessandri regime the exchange rate did not so move, at least in the early years. Nonetheless, its dollar-deposit and dollar-bond systems must be considered as a first step toward the protection of the savings of the public, even though the particular choice of dollars as the denomination in which the bonds and deposits were expressed was an unwise one for a variety of reasons.

Also under Alessandri came the introduction of savings and loan institutions. These institutions pay interest rates of 4 percent to their depositors and charge approximately 7 percent to their borrowers, but the face value of the deposit or the loan is regularly readjusted to reflect the change in the general price level. These institutions effectively provide an inflation-safe form of saving. They also provide a way of eliminating the inflationary benefit which borrowers traditionally have received in Chile, and enable the savings and loan institutions to make long-term loans without themselves incurring inflationary risks. However, one may reasonably ask whether the particular use to which the funds garnered by savings and loan institutions were put was a very high priority use from the standpoint of the economic development of Chile. In point of fact, these funds are reserved for mortgage loans for essentially middle- and upper-class housing. There is as yet no direct counterpart to the savings and loan institutions for mobilizing inflation-protected funds from savers and chan-neling them into industrial development or into other uses more directly conducive to economic development than luxury and semiluxury housing.

Under the present Chilean administration two additional steps have been taken: savings deposits in the State Bank have been made readjustable, and readjustable central bank bonds have been issued. Additional measures have recently been taken which will permit the lending of some of these funds on a readjustable basis.

These recent steps should be applauded, but there is still a substantial gap in the capital market of Chile. What is needed is to generalize the scheme of readjustable deposits so as to reach the entire saving and borrowing public. This can be done by opening a way for all banks to receive savings and time deposits that are readjustable, and to permit them to use the proceeds to finance industrial activities by medium- or long-term loans. Alternatively, industrial development banks might be established and explicitly charged with the above functions. It is unfortunate that, even after several years of discussion of pro-posals of these types, no concrete results in this direction have yet been achieved.

However, it should be noted that under the present administration, while depositors in accounts other than State Bank savings accounts have still lost purchasing power on their savings, bank borrowers are at present paying a positive real rate of interest on their borrowings. This particular end has been accomplished in large measure through a special tax levied by the government on bank loans—a tax which is sufficient, in conjunction with the interest rate charged by the banks, to force borrowers to pay a genuinely positive price for the credit that they obtain.

Turning now to the foreign exchange market, I would like to emphasize the key role that the exchange rate plays in governing the pattern of development of any economy. In essence, the exchange rate is at one and the same time a protective device for local production and also a stimulator of exports. If a country keeps its exchange rate low, it places in jeopardy not only its industries which compete with imports but also its actual and potential export industries. Of course, if a country follows the policy of keeping an exchange rate too low, it will tend to import too much and export too little, and the consequent balance of payments problem must somehow be solved. The traditional solution to this in Chile has been to restrict imports and thus create artificial incentives to establish new and often economically unjustified domestic industries, which, whether inefficient or not, appear to have tremendous staying power once established.

Two sectors have been neglected in this historic pattern of Chilean exchange-rate policy and of reaction by protective import restriction. The first such sector has been agriculture. Here the motivation has been to keep low the prices of certain key agricultural products, some of which are important in the cost of living of Chilean consumers. When the exchange rate is kept low, and commodities like wheat and meat are imported into Chile at correspondingly low prices in domestic currency, Chilean farmers face a strong disincentive to produce these products. Exchange-rate policy has thus contributed to the relative stagnation—or perhaps better put, the relatively low rate of growth—of Chilean agricultural production.

Nontraditional exports have suffered from Chile's exchange-rate policy in two ways. They have suffered from the exchange rate often being held constant for long periods of time while internal prices and costs rose, thus to erode profits and eventually convert them into substantial losses. The erratic relationship between exchange rates and the level of internal prices and costs has also led investors to be very reluctant to invest in industries whose future is closely tied up with the government's exchange-rate policy. The second way in which Chile's exchange-rate policy has been harmful to nontraditional exports is through the low average relationship which the exchange rate itself has borne to the level of internal prices and costs. That is to say, not only has the exchange rate fluctuated in relation to internal prices but also its average level has been too low to attract significant resources to the development of new and nontraditional export industries. That there are industries which could be expanded very profitably for Chile is beyond doubt. In agriculture Chile has a great advantage in the production of citrus fruits, other fruits, and wine. Particularly in the area of fresh fruits the geographic location of Chile in the Southern Hemisphere is an enormous advantage, because Chile's harvest comes at a time when fruits are out of season in the major producing centers of the Northern Hemisphere. There is no doubt in my mind that, given a more economically appropriate exchange-rate policy, Chile should be able to develop exports of citrus fruits far surpassing those which Israel has been able to achieve in the last decade or so. In industry as well, Chile has the capacity to become a significant exporter of iron and steel, cellulose, and paper and paper products. Some degree of exportation of all these products has been achieved in the past in spite of very unfavorable exchange-rate policies. Much more, however, could be achieved if more appropriate exchange policies were followed.

The present government has followed in one sense a better

exchange-rate policy than its predecessor, though in another sense not. On the positive side, it has maintained a stable exchange rate relative to internal prices and costs. This has been done by permitting the exchange rate to rise *pari passu* with increases in the internal price level. On the negative side, this stability has been achieved at a low level. The previous administration had permitted a very substantial deterioration in the exchange rate relative to the internal price level. Thus, when the Frei administration took office, the relationship was more prejudicial to the development of new export industries than had been the case on the average during the Alessandri administration. It is a matter of credit that the situation was not permitted to deteriorate further and that the drastic oscillations of the exchange rate-price level relationship, characteristic of earlier years, have been avoided. It is, on the other hand, unfortunate that the level of the relationship has not been significantly raised. (It must be pointed out that recent developments in the world copper market have placed Chile in a very favorable balance-of-payments situation and that under these circumstances the failure to bring about a substantial rise in the exchange rate is understandable. Nonetheless, as copper prices fall and more normal levels are approached, it is highly desirable that these movements be reflected in a rising exchange rate rather than in the traditional tightening of restrictions on imports.)

I turn now to the question of inflation and stabilization policy. Chile's endemic inflation requires no further description or elaboration. But we can ask what has been the fundamental cause of the inflation. Has it been a wage-push phenomenon? So say the industrialists, who justify their price increases as having been predominantly forced by wage increases. So, also, say the so-called structuralists, a group which is politically substantially to the left of the industrial community. The structuralists argue that bottlenecks and shortages in the economy, particularly in the agricultural sector and in the foreign sector, cause price increases which lead trade unions to demand wage increases, thus to initiate an upward inflationary spiral. This is not the place to go into the details of this matter or into the ample evidence that exists on the subject. Suffice it to say that empirical evidence in favor of a wage-push hypothesis is simply not present in the Chilean case.

If it has not been wages, then what *has* been the predominant cause of inflation. One thing can be said with certainty: monetary expansion is absolutely essential for any continuing inflation. It is possible for a country to have some inflation without substantial monetary expansion, but that inflation will be limited and will not be a continuing phenomenon.

The fact that monetary expansion is essential for a continuing inflation does not, however, mean that blame for the inflation lies at the door of the Central Bank, which is the agency of the Chilean government which actually prints new money. We must ask, rather, Why does the money supply expand? In many circumstances the Central Bank may be legally obliged to expand the money supply in favor of the government or in favor of the private sector. In point of fact the Chilean Central Bank is required to buy any obligations offered to it by the government, and has continually been so required in the past. Also at some times in the past the Central Bank has been required to finance the expansion of credit to the private sector.

In some stabilization attempts, based on a crude quantity-of-money focus, the prescription to fight inflation has been simply to stop the printing presses. These attempts have often neglected the fact that if the money supply stops expanding and the government keeps on borrowing from the Central Bank and the banking system as a whole, the only way that the banking system can accommodate the incremental loans to the government is by curtailing private sector credit. This in turn has, in the cases referred to, led to reductions in the level of output and of economic activity in the economy.

Thus, to keep the quantity of money in check without causing a decline in activity in the economy, the country must keep within reasonable limits the financing of fiscal deficits by means of printed money. In fact, the evidence is quite clear that the basic problem underlying Chile's inflation, at least in recent decades, has been that of excessively large fiscal deficits financed by the banking system.

This diagnosis of the problem has been well known to responsible Chileans for some time, including some of those who have been responsible for monetary and fiscal policies in earlier administrations. But in these earlier administrations the Chilean Congress was too divided to be able to act responsibly to curtail the fiscal deficits. The Alessandri administration had a wonderful chance to bring inflation essentially to a halt in 1960 and 1961. During these years the rate of inflation in Chile was below 10 percent per annum, and in that sense one can say that price stability had been almost achieved. Had the government moved during that time to rectify its underlying fiscal situation, the stage would have been set for a permanent solution. However, virtually nothing was done on the crucial fiscal front, and as a consequence inflation broke out once again in 1962 and has averaged well over 30 percent per year since then.

For many other reasons, but most importantly because a large fiscal deficit cannot be eliminated overnight, a gradual approach is preferable to a shock-treatment approach in dealing with an inflation like Chile's. Without the rectification of the fiscal deficits, the shock-treatment approach—as indicated above— necessarily entails the curtailment of credit to the private sector and consequently jeopardizes economic activity. The gradual slowing down of the rate of inflation as the fiscal situation is improved is a far preferable course to take. This is indeed what the present Chilean administration has been doing with notable success.

But once one recognizes that the stopping of the inflationary process will be gradual, one must also recognize the necessity to live with some degree of inflation for a period of years as this process runs its course. To live intelligently with inflation means to adopt policies which limit insofar as possible the deleterious effects which inflation has upon the economy. Such policies include, as has been indicated earlier, providing for the readjustability of bank deposits and of loans, and also of preventing the wild gyrations in the exchange rate-price level relationship which occur when the exchange rate is maintained stable for long periods while inflation drives internal prices strongly upwards. As I indicated earlier, the present Chilean administration has performed well on both of these scores.

Finally, let me make a few remarks on the overall growth prospects for the Chilean economy. In the first place, it is important to recognize that Chile's past growth record has really not been bad. Since 1940 the economy has grown at roughly 3.5 percent per annum overall, and at the rate of about 1.5 percent per capita per year. This is approximately what the United States has experienced on the average over more than half a century. And it is well to recall that until very recently this United States' experience was the envy of the great majority of the countries of the world.

While Chile's past history has not been bad, it certainly can be better. It can be better because what occurred in the past was in spite of a set of government policies—or lack of policies—which impaired the workings of the economy in a number of critical ways. We have indicated in this paper several key areas in which policy weaknesses have hampered the functioning and impeded the growth of the economy. The rationalization of economic policy is the essence of good planning, and this is exactly what has been absent in Chile for the whole postwar period up to the present. And this is what Chile is in fact getting from its present government—an intelligent coordination of economic policies on a number of different fronts, together with basic social and educational reforms which, though they do not have immediate influence on the rate of growth, will certainly have a positive effect in the future. I am highly optimistic that Chile will for the immediately foreseeable future be able to establish a record of economic performance which is substantially superior to what has occurred in the past, so long as its policy continues to evolve along the lines that have been signaled in the first two years of the Frei administration.

Part III:
Sociological Aspects

6: THE PEOPLE'S ROLE IN THE REVOLUTION
Luis Scherz-García

In 1964, after a spectacular electoral victory, Christian Democracy gained control of the government of Chile. This event was inextricably intertwined with a sudden increase in the number of voters participating for the first time in the political life of the nation. It is safe to say that the majority of this new electorate, until then existing in a kind of political exile, felt itself in accord with the ideological and programmatic postulates of Christian Democracy and so supported it to carry out a revolution, the Revolution in Freedom.

The ideology that enables Christian Democracy to identify itself with a huge sector of the people consists of an interpretative view of the revolutionary process and of its essential elements. The principal task of my exposition will consist precisely in showing the role which that ideology, a communitarian one, assigns to the people in the revolution. To achieve this purpose, I will place myself both outside the ideology and within it. In one instance I will consider it as a phenomenon which I must analyze by empirical methods; in the other I will consider it as a living thing which I must try to understand through empathy and inner comprehension. The two perspectives will be tied together in my presentation, but, nevertheless, the latter will predominate over the former and will frequently lead me to adopt the tone and peculiarities of political language itself, much as a Christian Democrat militant would do if addressing his party comrades. Finally, admitting the existence of a variety of tendencies within the ideological resources of communitarianism, I will concentrate on presenting that tendency which I per-

93

sonally consider representative of its revolutionary spirit.[1] The following exposition is to be regarded as a sample of the ideological views of communitarianism, presented in its own terms without the distortions of a mere external analysis which might show with great precision a lifeless anatomy, but not the vital vibrations of its rich reality.

THE REVOLUTION IN FREEDOM AND
THE STAGES IMPLIED IN IT

All revolution is a process of radical and intensive change by means of which the replacement of the most essential aspects of a given social system is sought. It does not deal merely with the modifying or substituting of some pieces or mechanisms of the system in order that the system may better fulfill its functions; nor with the alteration of the number of activities and the manner of carrying them out in order to better achieve traditional goals. Through revolution the structure, functions, and central objective of the system change, and thereby the system itself changes in its essential aspects. Reforms, despite their intensity and speed, change only parts and functions of a system, never its basic aim and meaning.

To facilitate the examination of the revolution, we may distinguish in it three main stages: first, a conflict, or disintegration of the traditional system; then, a period of transition from conflict to integration (brought about by the revolutionists' take-over of political power); and, finally, integration or consolidation of the new system. Regarding the Revolution in Free-

---

[1] By examining the corresponding proceedings of seminars programmed by the *Instituto de Estudios Políticos* (IDEP) of the Latin American Christian Democracy, located in Chile, it is possible to find the basic elements which serve as points of departure of our presentation. See especially the Proceedings of the *Seminario Internacional sobre la Propiedad* (Las Vertientes, February 1966); *Preseminario sobre la Visión Comunitaria de la Economía* (Millahue, June 1966); *Preseminario sobre la Visión Comunitaria del Derecho* (Las Vertientes, September 1966); *Seminario Nacional sobre la Visión Comunitaria de la Educación* (Las Vertientes, November 1966).

dom, the first stage has already taken place and the second is in progress. Our purpose will be to explain and illustrate, in this paper, the development of the various stages and the eventual outcome of the third stage. Along with our analysis we plan to show the role of the people, the party, the government, and the ideology itself in the revolutionary process.

THE PEOPLE: SEARCHING FOR SOCIAL POWER

The existence of groups which until 1964 were almost totally excluded from political activities leads to the further discovery that political marginality was only one visible indicator of an almost total exclusion of these groups from the life of the nation. Before 1964 two-thirds of Chile was to all appearances excluded from economic benefits, was borderline insofar as an equitable distribution of social prestige and stimulus was concerned, and was excluded from education and participation in political decisions: in other words, two-thirds of the populace lacked meaningful social power. A whole nation was cut off from that area where the benefits of social life were shared. In fact, a kind of vast shadow nation, consisting apparently of a passive mass, existed alongside an official nation which in its more integrated core comprised only a minority of the country's population. The official, juridically established society might be likened to the cone of a volcano, ignorant of its gigantic, subterranean interior.

In the midst of this society dominated by the privileged or oligarchical minorities there arose problems and struggles, ideological disagreements, economic crises, labor conflicts, political instability: all these were signs of the growing disintegration and exhaustion of its vital possibilities. Viewed from afar, the Chilean nation nevertheless projected an image of a certain cohesion and unity. The great submerged society, on the other hand, seemed at first only a monstrous aggregate of persons and groups (of peasants and slum-dwellers), unaware of their mar-

ginal situation and their needs, living in a precritical and pre-
logical primitivism, an object of social action and not a subject
or agent of major changes. A closer examination of its characteristics, however, provided grounds for a less pessimistic appraisal
of its future prospects. Analytically there could be discerned
communitarian ways of life, molded spontaneously around
original values of the people. In their simple organizations it
was possible to find the imprint of a national character. In the
official society, on the contrary, the grotesque imitation of foreign ways of life stamped its culture as false and artificial. Its
basic institutions appeared to be modeled after those of Europe
and the United States.

It is, of course, impossible to draw a clear line between the
unofficial and the official nation; in the latter, certain less-
organized proletarian sectors, unlike those included in the most
powerful unions, seemed to live in an utterly marginal situation;
on the other hand, certain sectors, apparently participants in the
economic benefits of the "integrated" society, considered themselves ideologically excluded from it, an exclusion expressed by
their critical attitude toward social injustices. These rebel groups
were socially isolated, blocked in their political interests, and dis-
criminated against in the distribution of prestige and social
encouragement. Among their members were included professionals, university students, women (many of them well-to-do
economically), and intellectuals. All of them, along with important workers' groups, were considered part of the official society
but did not really belong to it inasmuch as they were committed
to its radical replacement. In their eyes the society then holding sway was absolutely inadequate to satisfy the needs and
aspirations of the people.

The entire social system, therefore, included both those participants who followed the traditional rules of the game and
those who, either through necessity or choice, did not seek the
goals the rules prescribed. The social system presented itself
as a complex of forces in unstable equilibrium. The marginal
groups at first seemed unaware of their situation and of the fact

that their interests were opposed to those of the dominant minority. An ideological impulse would, however, serve to transform the vague consciousness of basically similar social conditions shared by these marginal groups into an acute awareness of them.

THE ORGANIZATION OF THE IDEOLOGICAL VANGUARD OF THE PEOPLE

A constellation of ideas which interprets reality, which incorporates the most enduring values of the large aggregates alienated from the official power, and which assumes all the emotional burden of those who wish to change the established order, comes to be the first expression of the communitarian society toward which the Chilean revolution wants to lead. Through ideology an oppressed people begins to acquire a critical understanding of its situation, interests, and common objectives; in response to ideological motivation the people initiate their organization and struggle to achieve political power. The enlightened vanguard of the people emerges as a first institutional crystallization of the communitarian ideology. With it begins the initial concrete change in a structural sector of the traditional system.

Let us recall that about thirty years ago a group of university students founded a new party, outside the scheme of the traditional parties, designed to reveal the injustices and structural inadequacies of the prevailing social system, to interpret the aspirations of groups that lacked social cohesiveness, and to draw up guidelines for a new society inspired by the evangelical message. This first vanguard of searchers, interpreters, and demonstrators of authentic popular aspirations thereby established its identification with the oppressed and constituted the first organized expression of the new society. Such identity, guaranteed by a process of reciprocal influence, determined its force and conditioned its future. Stressing liberty and justice, *Falange Nacional* was born.

In this stage of seeking political power the breadth and richness of the movement's ideology[2] was coincidentally matched by the quality of its leadership. These leaders strategically promoted the integration of convergent forces, which finally led to the foundation of the Christian Democratic party: an instrument destined to attain political power, a vital one among all the social powers. Conflicts between the ideology of the Revolution in Freedom and the traditional ideologies (ranging from conservatism to Marxism) became intensified as the recent, historical presidential election approached. During the electoral campaign the debate flared into the open and continued for almost two years before the presidential balloting. During this period of undoubted pedagogical value the candidates took the opportunity to make their ideological positions and programs (which were especially emphasized) known to the people. We believe the decisions, not to be completely discounted, that may have arisen from thoughtlessness, prejudice, fear, personal commitments, or economic pressures were of minor importance as compared to the many well-considered decisions taken in a critical spirit. A large combination of peasants, pobladores (slum-dwellers), unemployed, women, and young people of different social levels enjoyed this favorable civic environment.

[2] Since ideology is a "driving idea," its main role is to produce (or to detain) changes in the reality which it interprets. It is not as much a "grasping idea" of the examined reality as an "operating idea" either at the service of a still nonexisting reality (revolutionary ideology) or at the service of the preservation of the status quo (conservative ideology).

The ideological impulse of the revolution blows like a wind which not only intends to move the reality from its actual negative position toward an implicit position of new "normality" or order, but which moreover intends to bring it to a utopian situation. Although an unreachable position, it is functional for social change. For when the calm returns after the counterrevolutionary resistances are defeated, a new reality approaching the utopian position is reached. The need for ideological exaggeration perhaps can be clarified by a metaphor. Seeing an inclined tree, a gardener guided by a "nonideological" or static vision of reality would try to put it straight according to a vision of normality. He would put it perfectly vertical, but when left to itself, the tree would become inclined again. A gardener with ideological conscience would tend spontaneously to incline it in an opposite angle, and when free, it would reach the vertical position.

All had the chance to weigh and prepare their decisions in an atmosphere of free discussion. Finally, the presidential election itself provided a constitutional means of arriving at the decisive stage of the revolution:[3] the stage of transition from the oligarchical society to the communitarian society. Irresistibly pushing aside the traditional political power, the people assumed visible control of the whole society. The Christian Democratic government thus began its terms of office.

Could Communism likewise have won power through legal means? This is a perplexing question. Communism would certainly have succeeded if it had had a better understanding of the peoples' aspirations. But the presence of certain inhibiting factors in Marxist ideology—some essential, others secondary—decreased its strength and brought it to failure. The narrow, rigid ideology of Communism leads it to concentrate exclusively on the dichotomy between the poles of the economic situation: the workers versus the owners of capital. The more strategic and comprehensive dichotomy between those who exercise social power (of which economic power is only a part) and those who are denied such power is heavily disregarded by Communism.[4]

[3] The contribution of multiple factors or situations which converged to the success of the Christian Democratic candidature, such as the international prestige attained by Christian Democracy, the more progressive attitude assumed by the Church, and the fear of Communism in traditional sectors of society is not to be underestimated. Nevertheless, these and other situations did not, of course, escape ideological analysis, and it could be said that some of them were products of its strategy.

[4] The one-sided view of Marxism, stressing only the economic aspects of reality, leads it to consider industrial workers as the only genuine agents of the revolution they propose. Reality proves that the conflicts between capital and labor being institutionalized, the labor union, forgetting its proletarian mission, tends to follow a mere policy of "bread and butter" and of uplifting the prestige of the workers; thus, rather than a revolutionary agent, it is a negotiating agency of higher salaries. Several factors contribute to make more subtle the alienation of the laborers, take away from them their revolutionary impulses (notorious in the 1920's), and throw them, instead, into the orbit of pragmatic or reformist ideologies. In this way, increasing social mobility mentally places them in the immediately superior social strata. Their situation in their social level is like

THE PEOPLE: AGENT OR PATIENT OF THE REVOLUTION?

Christian Democracy has received from the people the power and the opportunity to bring about the transition to the communitarian society. The people have identified themselves ideologically and socially with the party and have elected a Christian Democratic government as the instrument to execute and administer the revolutionary process. For the past two years the present government has been carrying on this task. Forgetting for the moment its successes and failures, let us point out rather, in the light of the ideology, the meaning of this stage and the role which the people should play in it. We hope to indicate, therefore, the normative—the "ought to be"—guidelines that the ideology requires, in general, for the successful accomplishment of this phase. From this perspective the revolutionist may judge, if he wishes, how far his movement has progressed or has failed.

In the struggle toward the new society the party, as farsighted leader of the people, bears the responsibility for propagating its ideological impulse and mobilizing the society of the entire world behind it. At this stage the custody of the revolution's fulfillment, its control and orientation, is entrusted to the party. It is the principal institutional agent for planning the process of transition, for motivating the individual agents of the revolution, and for placing them, according to the rules of democratic

that of people in a bus; they get off at the proper opportunity or when the bus stop of a higher social position has been reached. In lessening the strength of the labor movement, the international guilds' organizations of the salary negotiation type, like the Inter-American Regional Workers' Organization, have directly or indirectly exerted considerable influence. The Latin American labor movement, especially that of the industrial worker, appears disorganized and deprived of force (save when it plays a true role of a political party as in Argentina).

Ideology results from an emotionally sanctioned union between a set of values and a changing reality. When reality changes, ideology has to be readjusted. Otherwise it would no longer be able to guide and motivate actions along the successive "here and now" of the revolutionary process. The one-sided view of reality gives the Marxist ideology the cohesion of a dogma but reduces its operative power.

planning, in the most strategic positions for efficient action, that is, in the government and other key institutions. Unity and efficiency in the coordinated actions of the people, the party, and the government is assured by unity in ideology. The elaboration of a common ideology is the central mission of a party which organizes in its ranks those members of the people with a keen revolutionary conscience. The fulfillment of this mission also assures the party's internal democracy and brings more flexibility to its disciplined action.

The communitarian society, toward the achievement of which the joint revolutionary effort of the people, party, and government aims, appears as a mosaic constructed according to a new design, particularly in those sectors that traditional society must abandon. The entire change of the social system must be guided by an ideological strategy—at once realistic, critical, and audacious—which will guarantee, on one hand, the popular character and force of the revolution and, on the other, the elimination of oligarchical resistance, even while it avoids unnecessary violence. Thus, in the first moment of victory the revolutionists should take advantage of the initial confusion of their adversaries and direct their efforts toward effecting radical and rapid changes in the economic, juridical, and educational fields, and toward replacing personnel holding key positions in the public administration.

We must recall that the revolutionary government is the government of those who were previously excluded from the social power but who now have attained power in the political realm. This is not the government of the oligarchy, or is it designed to serve that group. One of its aims is to destroy the oligarchy and take from it whatever social power it still retains. This is not to be considered revenge of any kind: the facts make clear that the revolution cannot be achieved without having first overcome certain obstacles, or without leaving some in an unsatisfactory situation through the loss of their privileges (especially economic). To eliminate such privileges does not mean loss of life in the Revolution in Freedom. According to this revolution respect for the human person and for his essential rights leads to justice, not to injustice.

All economic policies of the government are ideally subordinated to the overall purposes of the revolution. At the outset it is less crucial that economic indices rise than that the people remain loyal to their revolutionary tasks. Misery will not be overcome by means of a traditional or reformed economic structure, or substantially through the introduction of birth-prevention methods of population control. It will only be overcome by channeling the productive forces and sacrifices of the people through new structures constructed with their participation. The collapse of the oligarchical economic power, accelerated by the agrarian reform, should be turned to the immediate benefit of society's underprivileged members. In the opening stages it does not necessarily mean that all the country shall be reduced to the level of misery, and even less is it the intention to subsidize the present well-to-do producers so that from their abundance enough may be derived to fill the pockets of those in misery; but it certainly does matter that the country should witness at once the drastic elimination of the great social and economic discrepancies that exist among its inhabitants—a joint enterprise in which sacrifices are shared mutually. The dynamics of the revolution can only progress in an atmosphere of justice that results from the majority of a nation's people meeting the challenge of a common undertaking.

During this period the government, with all the resources of the state at its command, has a very direct and unavoidable responsibility to the people who elected it. Aware of their political power, the people strive to increase it and to transform it into permanent social power. From this viewpoint the government participates in the political power of the people, a participation gained through sporadic election activities; for its part the government operates as a multiplying and transforming device, with the goal of returning to the people that political force, increased and extended to other forms of social power. The task of organizing the people coincides with the redistribution of the social power.

Let us recall that the gradual incorporation of the people in the party and in the electoral nucleus of Christian Democracy reached the peak of its intensity during the presidential campaign. As an irrefutable witness to the action of the party and the enthusiasm of the people, it is a fact that thousands of electoral committees arose at that time in offices and factories, in the cities and farmlands, of the nation. In taking advantage of the situation created by these preliminary efforts, the business of the government, as directed by the party, should consist in institutionalizing many of these initiatives and in shaping transitional or community forms of life: *juntas vecinales*, cooperatives, unions (of farm and industrial workers), peasant commands, *asentamientos agricolas*, and youth groups. Politically, the task is to seek the legitimization of the *juntas vecinales* (local government assemblies formed around neighborhood units) and to try to have them constituted as basic cells of government endeavor. By opening the way to the communitarian enterprise, accelerating the agrarian reform, and facilitating the conditions for the development of a revolutionary labor-union movement, economic problems are attacked. In regard to education, by giving the means and instruments to the people for the expression of their own cultural message a culture of the revolution can be created. Juridically, the task can be accomplished by establishing the people as the judge of the transcendental decisions of the country. This is a prerequisite insofar as the oligarchy and its allies, supported by an obsolete juridical system and by unjust traditions, continue to offer opposition. All of these initiatives arise from the "automotion" of the people, since it is their own power which returns to them through the government's action. Without overlooking the eventual need to train and attend to the wants of the most deprived citizens in order to make use of their talents (through instruments like INDAP and *Promoción Popular*), each individual shall always be looked upon as an agent motivated by the fire of the ideology which nourishes him, an ideology which, in turn, is propagated by the party in a process of reciprocal interchange. Therefore, as a matter of principle the party can never excuse itself from the job of organizing the people. Such an endeavor shall be tactically stated in view of the circumstances.

The task of organizing the people touches directly upon their revolutionary role. Thus, we are obliged to make explicit the sense or meaning that the ideology bestows upon that role and to distinguish it from those pseudorevolutionary positions which may infiltrate the process of revolution itself. The way in which the question is phrased separates one position from the other. Communitarianism asks itself, What place shall each individual fill in the struggle to transform the society that he is trying to overcome? According to this way of wording it the people assume an active role in the revolutionary process which they themselves have brought into being. Only a non-revolutionary perception could formulate the question differently, that is, How can the people presently excluded from society be integrated into a milieu which has already been established but which still needs reforms in order to be consolidated? Or, how can the marginal man be socialized in order that he may assume civic responsibilities and be economically productive? Here is a whole group of problems arising from the pragmatic considerations of social survival and fundamentally deriving from a reformist rather than a revolutionary attitude toward the social structure, as well as from an erroneous interpretation of the true social values of the population which the reformers condescendingly plan to admit to the benefits of civilization.

Each option has a different meaning at the level of the persons themselves, their social relationships, and their values. A pseudorevolutionary or "development" position would conceive of society as divided between those who are agents (or actors) and those who are the objects (or receptors) of social action, the former exercising influence over the latter, who are thus gradually introduced into the realm of activity demanded by social life. There would then exist a rigid dualism or stratification between those who direct and those who are directed, those who are integrated and those who are excluded, those who are benefactors and those who are benefited. According to the revolutionary conception, on the other hand, the person should be considered both as the end and as the agent of the social process.

In the area of those social relationships which give life to the various institutions the developmentalism conception would fall back on organizing the people according to the guidelines of subordination or paternalism. Thus, each social unit or community would be subordinated to higher social organizations like the state, and the state in turn would be subordinated to systems of greater international power and influence. On the contrary, the revolutionary conception would seek to set up a system of guidelines proper to the cooperation of free entities and would try to coordinate activities according to the rational criteria of common benefit. From a cultural viewpoint, we will soon point out how the "development" position's technocratic and alienating vision is opposed to communitarian humanism. Where developmentalism is simply a servile imitation of a foreign way of life, communitarian humanism represents the authentic values of the people.

Then also there are two views concerning the role the mass of people may play in the process of change in Chile, and in all Latin America as well. One point of view favors incorporating the people into a reformed nucleus of present society by means of specific assistance programs and through tasks assigned according to the will of the benefactors. On another level this process would mean integrating the country according to a foreign frame of reference and subordinating it once and for all to the drive of foreign imperialisms. The other point of view would favor the integration and participation of the same people in their own revolutionary task by means of their own initiative and through their own advanced ideological organization. This would then be the process that on another level would contribute to the integration of a Latin American society centered around authentic values and constituted by free men organized in a communitarian way.

THE RESISTANCE TO THE COMMUNITARIAN REVOLUTION

In this stage of transition, ideology perhaps plays its most important role in the entire revolutionary process, since it must continually unmask the counterideology that stems from the displaced oligarchy. Through this counterideology a subtle attempt is made to infiltrate the minds of the revolutionaries and to confuse their actions in the hope that they may fall into pragmatic and opportunistic errors or into other temptations of a spurious character which may slow or undermine the revolution's progress. This oligarchical effort is launched after an intensive conflict has served to sharpen the ideological differences between the oligarchy and communitarianism. The announcement that the communitarian society will be integrated around a new set of values, and not around those that arise out of deals and compromises, stirs enormous resistance among the minorities who have been displaced and induces them to map out an involved strategy for defending their interests. What effects has this strategy had thus far on the development of the transitional stage?

It is our task, not to answer the question, but rather to divide it into additional questions which each revolutionist shall pose for himself with a critical mentality. What ideological positions are held by occupants of key positions in the public administration? In what measure do the reformists or "development" experts manage to control the national economy? Is the neo-capitalist training of the economists looked upon with concern, and what about the backward-looking education of lawyers at the universities? Does the party play its role of orienting the organization of the people in full freedom? The tentative answer to these and other questions may give us an indication of the progress of the counterrevolutionary effort. If the government forgets that the party is the voice of the people, and if the party loses its identification with them, the revolutionary process may become misshapen and stunted. The vitality and vigor of the party, which is the first institutional expression of the aspirations and motivations of the emerging people, is reflected and stimulated by the dynamism of its ideological positions. Once again, in the order of government it is ideology that lights the way; it is an enlightenment that is all the more intense in the degree that it is precise and unmistakable. Likewise, the program of the government is nothing more than a concrete expression of the ideology and is subject, therefore, to the variations and improvements which ideological orientations may demand for achieving the permanent goals of the revolution.

THE POPULAR CONTENT OF THE COMMUNITARIAN IDEOLOGY

The integrating or consolidating stage of the communitarian society may only be attained if the party remains loyal to its ideological mission by interpreting the people and orientating the government. Nevertheless, the third stage can never be considered as definitely ended; not even within this stage's development will all social tensions be eliminated. These will, however, lose their destructiveness and be transformed into seeds of human perfection by being fraternally institutionalized. Ideology, adjusted to the new realities which shall emerge, will show the way toward a fraternal society. It is fitting now to make explicit some of this society's values so that they may act as the stars helping the ship of revolution to navigate.

Embodied in a Latin American historical context, certain central features of the set of evaluations that occur jointly in the gospels, democracy, and science attain special force in the notion of communitarianism. These considerations were implicitly present in the aspirations of those who were formerly alienated. The high esteem with which many—especially women of diverse social conditions and youth—regard ethical values,[5] and

[5] The aversion against political corruption explains in great measure the popularity of the independent presidential candidature of Carlos Ibáñez del Campo 1952 and in lesser degree that of Jorge Alessandri in 1958.

the idealism and social consciousness of the governing leaders, indicate that religious aspirations have not died but live on as a survival of the evangelical message which certain superstitious practices have been unable to deform. Just as the exodus of agricultural laborers to the cities presupposes in many of them a critical attitude and an eagerness for active participation in planning their future, so does it underline their desire to contribute to the founding of a democratic life; paradoxically, this mentality is proper too—though more acute—to those who are disposed to stay in the agricultural areas for the purpose of bringing about the revolution in the farming environment. Among industrial workers, professionals, and university students the rational planning of activities according to a scale of priorities which is compatible with communitarian humanism enjoys a high esteem. Thus, ideology issues forth from reality itself in conjunction with permanent values or with a vital world vision of the universe and existence. The content of the evangelical message carried beyond the context of clericalism and closer to an emphasis on human brotherhood is not foreign to communitarianism. A love for a more authentic democracy, devoid of the paternalistic approach of closed groups and the permanent abusive concentration of social power, is not foreign to communitarianism. Nor are scientific endeavors[6] alien to this

---

[6] The application of the rational effort of man over the world of nature has carried him gradually to master it, to overpass the times when he should submit himself totally to its empire or to adapt himself to it. In overcoming the challenges which confront him in social life, the impact of rationality has been of lesser extent; but the moment will come in which man will predict with greater precision the consequences of its policies and reach better the concretion of the values which are more important for him. Nor in the social area, however, will man be able to overcome a barrier of limitations connected with his invariable human nature; but he will come to know them and to look for the elements to control them. He will grasp with greater clarity the "compressions" and "decompressions" to which the atmosphere of social life occasionally submits him, the alienative pressure that injustice exerts upon his personality, the anomic vacuum to which bureaucratization and urban anonymity may reduce him. For good or bad, a world of possibilities open themselves to the creative spirit of human beings. Those who may believe in the supreme value of brotherhood can elaborate

concept, for by means of these, reality may be diagnosed, explained, and mastered, thereby to pave the way to the realization and consolidation of the revolution.

These permanent values, besides helping define the central goals of the new social system, project themselves and give meaning to all the undertakings of government, the economy, law, and education. In all these fields the ideology remains faithful to its guideline and shows perpetually that the search for the common good is primarily a search, not for the happiness of all, but for the redemption of groups menaced by alienation from fraternal attention; it is among these latter groups that social injustice is found, and it is the duty of the communitarian society to eliminate all the sources, actual and potential, that permit an easy abuse of social power. Also, the state is considered a social instrument that shall be limited in its attributions, the more so as the third stage advances. Nevertheless, its powerful presence is considered indispensable for some time for the purposes of accomplishing the desired changes in structures and of retaining the necessary vigilance over the development of popular initiatives. In the economic area the ideology insists upon the communitarian forms of working the land and engaging in industry, and in the realm of law it demands pedagogically sound norms so that the exercise of solidarity may acquire relevance. Thus from the ethical imperative of communitarianism arises the demand that no person or group of persons shall be treated as objects of dominion or exploitation by others and also that property and other economic resources cannot be used to establish a subjugation of man by his neighbor.

In the educational field it emphasizes the propagation of revolutionary values by seeking the formation of an autonomous, fraternal, critical, and creative man. Its concept of man,

their models of social revolution challenging the historical determinisms or the pretended laws of unilineal evolution or "development," and trust, for the concretion of their projects, more in intelligence than in violence. And as always ideology will be the fuel and the rudder of the action.

founded upon the richness of the person's creative possibilities, publicly opposes any demeaning of the individual and emphasizes personal merit rather than the merits of family, race, class, or any other qualification; granting the value of rational and critical attitudes, it rejects the merely mechanical discipline. Social relations, whether in the realm of labor or any other area, are seen as expressions of the supreme value of brotherhood. Lastly, conscious that each institution will provide the covering shelter for the entire man, the ideology avoids the extreme functional specializations of the social organizations; it strives rather to render each person capable of engaging in dialogue with others and of feeling at home in activities different from his own.[7] The communitarian society emerges as the "community of free men," constituting at the same time "the community of communities."[8]

Recognition of the successive stages for reaching the communitarian society forms an essential part of the revolutionary endeavor. Within the stage of integration this process will not cease, because from the profound experience of fraternal living-together shall emerge the infinitely progressive goals that mankind shall pose for itself in the future. The society of the people

[7] If we take concepts familiar to the scholar of the social sciences, we may describe the constellation of values of a society (at least in its more formal aspects, not in its content itself) through a set of prevalent options of an ethical type, before dilemmas posed by the action. A capitalist society would differentiate from a communist one, and both from a communitarian society, by different combinations and tones of their answers to a group of such dilemmas. If we adopt the dilemmas presented by Talcott Parsons (mediatism vs. immediatism, individual interest vs. collective interest, universalism vs. particularism, ascription vs. achievement, specificity vs. diffuseness) in the communitarian society, we see that along with the value bestowed upon rationality, the common good, personal merit (in public affairs), and a universal ethic, also the limitation of the functional specificity of the institutions is considered important (by introducing in them an optimal degree of diffuseness). In this way the communitarian production enterprise is not only a society of economic actors but, overall, a community of persons conscious of their essential dignity and of the possibilities of interchanging roles among themselves.

[8] See the inaugural speech of Jaime Castillo Velasco, director of IDEP, in the seminars mentioned above.

is none other than that multitude of persons disposed to reach the highest goals in improving their human condition: individuals aware of their intrinsic limitations and of the external challenges which shall be continually overcome, today on the level of vital needs, tomorrow in the realm of spiritual life. Where the people are, there man confronts, firsthand, his essential or ontic deprivation, his thirst for the absolute; but this is also the place where his spirit of solidarity impels him to aid first the weak and then the strong, and to inspire them all to fulfill their personal destinies.

Thus, there will be no final stage; once one challenge has been met, another will appear, and when this obstacle has been overcome, there will arise new ones, and so on without end. Man is like Sisyphus, the mythological figure condemned to roll a rock up a steep hill in Hades and only have it roll back again to the bottom. Sisyphus is the people; Sisyphus is man. Nevertheless, the people do conquer the peak, though when they do, another peak emerges. The man who takes part in a communitarian society is not the satisfied bourgeois, nor is he one who rests on his laurels, satisfied with an aim achieved, nor is he one who has made an eternity out of time. This whole dynamic conception of the communitarian revolution, from which all human revolution finds its nourishment, blossoms from the message of Christ. The communitarian society is none other than the unceasing search for the incarnation of the evangelical brotherhood, a society open to the creative ingenuity of man, since it can never be totally realized in time.

The foregoing presents the role of the people in the revolution according to the communitarian ideology. In the language that I have used, excepting the unavoidable sociological terms, I have tried to point out the symbolism of this ideology, a symbolism which decisively separates it from the ideological varieties of capitalism and socialism. I repeat once again that this exposition should be considered as only one among many possible presentations of an ideology which is still in the process of assuming a more definite profile.

7: IDEOLOGY AND PRACTICAL LABOR POLITICS

Henry A. Landsberger

THE ROOTS OF CHRISTIAN DEMOCRACY'S LABOR POLICY[1]

1. THE CRITICAL PLACE OF LABOR POLICY IN THE CHRISTIAN DEMOCRATIC PROGRAM

Both ideological—indeed, idealistic—commitments and political realities have shaped Christian Democratic labor policy from its earliest days. It should be recalled that the party was founded in late 1938 as a protest by a breakaway group of young Conservatives against what they considered the double failure of the traditional parties of the Right and, in particular, of their own Conservative party. At the level of practical politics the Conservative party's Gustavo Ross had just lost the presidential elections of 1938 to the candidate of the Popular Front, the Radical party's Pedro Aguirre, supported by Communists, Socialists, and other parties of the Left. In the eyes of the young

[1] The author recognizes that the statistical information in this paper is limited in scope, for although the statistical services of the Chilean government are among the best in Latin America, data on labor in Chile is still not extensive. Sr. Claudio Fuchs and Professor Emilio Morgado V., both of the Department of Industrial Relations of the Institute of Administration (INSORA), University of Chile, were in part responsible for providing me with the information I requested. Information on pending bills, legislation already approved, and so on, were kindly and expeditiously provided by the Chilean Embassy and the Ministry of Labor in Chile. Their personnel, as well as my friends in INSORA, have my deepest appreciation.

Falangistas,[2] however, that political failure was only a reflection of a second, more fundamental, failure at the level of ideology: that of refusing to accept the teachings of Popes Leo XIII and Pius XI. Instead of moving toward the philosophy of the papal social encyclicals, in which the material ambitions of the rich would be curbed by giving greater recognition to the needs of workers and, reluctantly, more power to the state, the Conservative party under the guidance of such influential men as Hector Rodriguez de la Sotta had in the mid-1930's increasingly turned toward a defense of the very private capitalism so vigorously condemned in *Rerum novarum* and *Quadragesimo anno*. It was this error in ideology and in ideals which, according to the young Christian Democrats, had lost the Conservative party the support of the economically weaker sectors of the population, who therefore combined under two banners equally odious to the Falange: on the one hand, that of Marxist socialism and Communism, and, on the other, that of Radicalism, tinged —according to the Falange—with outmoded anticlericalism, atheism, Masonic obscurantism, and sterile statism. It was the goal of the Christian Democratic party to rescue the weaker sectors of Chilean society from the ideological errors and the political control of both Left and Right.

While it was necessary for the new party to formulate a program which would appeal to these popular sectors more than the existing programs of the extreme left and the Radical party, it was at the same time necessary for it not to frighten away what might be called the "gently progressive" center of Chile. A program had to be fashioned which would be sufficiently novel to appeal to a growing stratum of young intellectuals and professionals who responded to idealism and ideology as well as self-interest and who were needed so that they might form the organizational backbone of the party. As in the poorer sectors of Chilean society, many of these intellectuals and profes-

[2] The name of the Christian Democratic party until 1957—despite their hostility, from the very beginning, to the Spanish Falange of General Francisco Franco.

sionals preferred a Marxist formula and were therefore unreachable to the Falange. But also like their poorer fellow citizens, there was another, very substantial group who did not like what they suspected to be the harshness inherent in the Marxist formula and preferred an ideology which promised humanism in method and in immediate result, as well as humanism in the long run, only the latter of which Marxism was seen as providing. The founders and present leaders of the Christian Democratic party were themselves such men, and they appealed to men like themselves. The program they formulated therefore had strong idealistic and humanistic undertones, eschewed violent revolution for all practical internal purposes, and contained many practical measures designed to capture the interest of the mass voter.

2. SUBTLETIES AND COMPLICATIONS

While ideology and practical politics dictated that the program of the Chilean Democratic party favor the poorer sectors of Chilean society over the traditional landowning elite and even over the more modern commercial and banking interests, that formula alone could be only the crudest policy guide. The underprivileged of Chile are not, after all, an internally homogeneous mass, clearly separated from the rich. They are a group of many different elements. The continuum of disadvantaged within Chilean society begins as high as the potentially vigorous entrepreneur who finds it difficult to obtain bank credit because he does not have the family connections of a less entrepreneurial individual, even though the latter uses for consumption expenditures credit which the former would have used for the expansion of production. Perhaps the continuum includes the eager and competent young technician or professional who can obtain neither the scholarship for foreign study nor the position in a ministry which would allow him to be productive, because a less competent professional who has connections with the Establishment obtains them. Another gradation of the continuum of disadvantaged might be the ordinary white-collar worker in banks and public agencies who would like to do a technically competent job but cannot because less effective individuals, placed in their positions by family influence or party machines, make it impossible. Then come key groups of skilled blue-collar workers, such as railwaymen, who are underprivileged when compared with some groups but not with others. This also applies to blue-collar workers in strategic positions, such as copper miners. Descending more in terms of economic and social status, the scale includes factory workers, by no means at the bottom of the scale because they have a relatively steady job and are covered by various income security benefits and social services. Beyond these it shades gradually into the clearly underprivileged peasant and those urban masses whose occupational situation is insecure and whose social deprivation can be clearly measured in terms of absence of education and, in particular, incredibly poor housing and health conditions.

Since these groups differ very considerably in their degree of deprivation, a dilemma arises which has faced all societies—including Britain—seeking to redistribute income and institute a welfare state. What is given to one subgroup among the underprivileged is taken from another, at least in the sense that these particular benefits are not distributed among it as they might have been. The dilemma is, of course, not only moral and economic but also political. Yet it is in our opinion essential to an understanding of the labor policy of the Christian Democratic party to recognize that it has been in the extraordinarily fortunate position that political and moral considerations have pushed toward choosing the same horn of the dilemma! For the party faces a situation in which the most privileged among the least privileged (many of the professionals, white-collar workers, and workers in sectors critical to the national economy) already owe allegiance to previously established ideologies and political parties—the Marxists and the Radical party. These sectors are in part, therefore, not subject to being moved by the Christian Democrats. But Popular Action Front (FRAP) and the Radicals, while promising much, have in fact done least for the very bottom strata of Chilean society, especially the peasant. Whatever the cause and the justification for the priorities of Radicals and Marxists, the urban and rural poor are less committed to any of the old party organizations than most of the blue-collar and white-collar elite. In fact, peasants have only recently begun to awaken politically and are therefore more accessible to a newcomer on the Chilean scene as is the Christian Democratic party (PDC).

Thus, both for idealistic reasons and for reasons of voter appeal and practical politics, "labor policy" for the PDC—and now also for its rivals on the left—has been necessarily much more complicated than working out a program for organized labor in the narrow sense, that is, that relatively privileged sector of the poor which is in trade unions, employees' federations, and so on. A program had to be formulated which would limit the various benefits given to the elite sectors of labor, both because the needs of that sector were not as intense as those of many other groups and because, from a political point of view, not many votes could be expected from a sector which was relatively small numerically, partly committed elsewhere, and likely to decrease in importance with the politization of new, larger, and poorer sectors. Labor policy in the narrow sense of what to do about *organized* labor is, therefore, best visualized either as a subordinate part or, indeed, as a competitor with the government's program of aid to the previously unorganized poor.

The latter program, called *Promoción Popular*, is a most significant indication that the Christian Democratic party and its government have realized that for moral, political, and economic reasons the time has come to address the genuinely underprivileged in Chile. The essence of *Promoción Popular* is the organization on a geographic basis of that mass of the most extremely poor who—just as Saul Alinsky has realized in the United States—cannot be marshaled in organizations based on occupation. Parts of the present government's program which will be discussed below, such as the policy of income redistribution and certain aspects of minimum wage policy, should also be visualized as part of *Promoción Popular* in a broad sense. They serve fundamentally to elevate the economic and social status of these most underprivileged masses, while at the same time, of course, winning supporters for the Christian Democratic party. (Whether the latter effect is intentional we need not discuss here: it is the kind of question about motives which no one will ever resolve.) In any case, *Promoción Popular* and policy toward organized labor must be seen as separate, and in part competing, aspects of Christian Democratic labor policy in the largest sense of the word.

3. Goals[3]

The Christian Democratic party's labor policy, as formulated before the election, contained seven goals—four of which were quite explicit and three of which, although less explicit, were equally important. The four explicit general objectives dealt with the poor as a whole in relation to the rest of society: (1) stability of employment (in other words, the equivalent of a full-employment policy as accepted by Britain and the United States after World War II); (2) the maintenance of a stable price level (an end to inflation); (3) a progressive increase in the share of national income going to labor; and (4) minimum wages and salaries (indeed, we would presume, minimum incomes) which would be *vitales*, that is, livable, sufficient for a decent level of subsistence. Less formally stated was a fifth general goal which, when explicitly recognized, makes several of the more specific programs of the Christian Democratic government comprehensible: (5) an increase in the power of the worker vis-à-vis his environment in the the most general sense

[3] A "Memorandum sobre politica laboral y de seguridad social par el Congreso del Partido Democrata Cristiano," dated August 9, 1966, contains an excellent summary of statements on labor policy contained in the so-called "White Paper," (a summary of the program of the Frei government, issued in late 1964), as well as relevant sections of the "Blue Book" which was presented to the First Congress of Christian Democratic Professionals and Technicians in 1964.

of that term, but particularly vis-à-vis his economic environment. If our previous analysis is correct, however, two further major goals must have been in the minds of those who formulated the specifics of the party's program, both before and after the 1964 election, although they are clearly less explicit and might be less readily acknowledged. One of these must have been (6) to increase economic equality within the whole sector of the poor, thereby reducing the relative privilege of its best-off sectors; and the other, (7) to increase the political and personal freedom among the poorest individuals and subgroups within the larger underprivileged sector, a freedom from domination not only by the oppressors of the Establishment but by better-off members of the poor themselves. This goal is understandable both in terms of an ideological attachment on the part of Christian Democrats to the ideal of individual freedom and in terms of the political realities and balance of power in the organized labor movement with which the party must deal. President Frei seemed to acknowledge both the existence of these less explicitly formulated policies, and the practical difficulties of pursuing them, when he said in an address to the party on the occasion of the second anniversary of his government: "It is easy to adopt a social policy which gives to and courts certain groups of professionals, or certain middle-class groups, or certain groups of industrialists, leaving in misery and infamy a million and a half workers who are not organized."[4]

PROGRAMS AND ACCOMPLISHMENTS

Specific programs and projects to implement these general goals were in some instances ready before the election. Others have been more definitively formulated since 1964, and others are still being discussed.

[4] "Discurso del Presidente Frei con motivo de celebrar el segundo aniversario de su gobierno, en presencia de dirigentes y miembros del Partido Democrata Cristiano, en el Teatro Caupolican," Presidencia de la Republica, Secretaria de Prensa, November 4, 1966, Santiago, Chile.

1. FULL EMPLOYMENT

Both before the presidential election of September, 1964, and in the months immediately afterward there seemed to be a dangerous lack of a specific program for the expansion of industrial employment in Chile. In other words, an outsider could see no specific plans for "industrialization." In part such a void could be justified on the basis that the government's very concrete project for increasing copper production, and thereby increasing the availability of foreign exchange, would automatically make available the investment funds necessary to create job opportunities. However, together with agrarian reform, industrialization had been promised as one of the pillars of the Frei government, and, promise or no, it was essential for a successful labor policy. The goal of the minimum livable wage for everyone, for example, cannot be reached unless a majority of the population have jobs in which they are sufficiently productive to warrant the payment of a livable wage.

Specific figures on unemployment and the expansion of employment for the country as a whole and for the industrial sector are not now available and are unlikely to appear for some time. But some direct information on employment in Santiago can be presented, as well as indirect evidence on the country as a whole. These statistics can be used to gain overall impressions of what is happening, but it would be dangerous to regard them as conclusive.

The general employment situation in the greater Santiago area, and industrial employment in particular, was moderately encouraging by the end of 1966, as may be seen from Table I. In 1966 an increase of 42,000 in employment absorbed almost the entirety of a massive increase of 50,000 in the total labor force (thereby to prevent all but a very small—and possibly insignificant—increase in unemployment from 3.9 to 4.3 percent) after the year 1965 had already seen a labor-force increase of 50,000 completely absorbed in employment. (Chile's rate of population growth results in an annual growth in the work force

TABLE I

WORK FORCE, EMPLOYMENT AND UNEMPLOYMENT IN GREATER SANTIAGO (IN 000'S AND %), 1961–1966

	1961 (December)		1962 (December)		1964 (December)		1965 (December)		1966 (December)	
	Work Force	% Unemployed	Work Force	% Unemployed	Work Force	% Unemployed	Work Force	% Unemployed	Work Force	% Unemployed
TOTALS	749.8	4.2	784.5	4.3	799.6	4.1	852.6	3.9	903.3	4.3
Agriculture	5.8	—	7.6	—	7.6	—	7.1	—	8.1	—
Extractive industries (mining, etc.)	4.1	—	1.7	—	2.2	—	2.8	—	3.9	—
Industry	212.5	5.7	212.7	5.1	223.6	5.0	247.2	4.2	260.6	4.1
Construction	47.9	10.7	46.1	16.1	55.6	15.7	56.2	10.3	50.9	15.6
Commerce	114.4	3.9	130.6	2.5	128.8	2.5	130.9	2.9	141.1	3.5
Transport, communications, and public utilities	52.3	3.0	51.1	4.5	50.2	3.5	52.7	4.1	64.3	6.3
Government services and finance	56.4	2.2	61.7	2.4	63.4	1.3	68.6	1.7	78.4	1.9
Personal services	132.7	1.7	151.4	1.7	130.2	2.6	137.3	2.9	148.8	4.0
Other services	117.2	3.3	116.9	4.4	132.2	2.4	142.8	3.2	136.9	2.0
Activities not well defined	1.1	—	1.0	—	—	—	0.2	—	—	—
Looking for work for the first time	5.5	—	3.8	—	5.7	—	6.9	—	10.3	—

(*Source:* Instituto de Economía, Universidad de Chile, *Ocupación y Desocupación: Gran Santiago,* December 1961–1966.)

of between 50,000–70,000.) Particularly noteworthy is the fact
that 14,000 members of the new labor force—more than one-
third—were absorbed by the industrial sector without any increase in unemployment there. It seems that employment
opportunities did not keep pace fully, however.

There clearly was considerable unemployment in the construction industry (an increase from 10.3 to 15.6 percent); there
was an increase in the labor force in "Personal services" which
may not be healthy (although this is offset in part by a decrease
in "Other services"); and the increase in "Transport, communications; and public utilities" is difficult to explain. Moreover,
early figures for 1967 show an overall increase in unemployment
to levels of 5 and 6 percent.

Other evidence on employment in Chile as a whole shows
that industrial production in manufacturing went up by at
least 5 percent in 1965 and that it had exceeded, by the end
of November 1966, the production of the corresponding eleven
months of 1965 by over 7 percent.[5] Such evidence is only indirect, however, since an increase in *production* may not necessarily bring with it an increase in *employment* if the increased
production is obtained through more intensive use of capital.
The great optimism shown by President Frei in his address to
the party on November 4, 1966,[6] therefore, should be viewed
with caution insofar as its implications for full employment are
concerned, although his optimism was clearly justified from
other points of view. President Frei referred to the opening of
a large number of plants: artificial fiber in Constitución and
Arauco; four new chemical plants in various parts of the country; copper refineries and new industries using refined copper
in the north. He also mentioned the large number of applications for permission to import machinery currently submitted

[5] "Indice de producción industrial manufacturera, mes de Noviembre de 1966,"
Dirección de Estadística y Censos, January, 1967, Santiago, Chile.
[6] "Discurso del Presidente Frei con motivo de celebrar el segundo aniversario
de su gobierno, en presencia de dirigentes y miembros del Partido Democrata
Cristiano, en el Teatro Caupolican," Presidencia de la Republica, Secretaria de
Prensa, November 4, 1966, Santiago, Chile.

to the Central Bank; plans for expansion by large and small industries, particularly textiles; and the substantial number of factories then working three shifts. It is most likely that such developments do in fact signify an expansion of highly productive industrial employment. Nevertheless, some of the expansion does seem to have occurred in industries which use relatively little labor, which makes it difficult to be sure that the increase in industrial production will be sufficient to keep pace with the rising labor force. In any case, it should not be expected that the rise in employment will be equal to the increase in value of manufacturing, since that would indicate no rise in productivity per worker, something which is neither likely nor desirable.

In summary, then, attention should be drawn to the fact that while a systematic and explicit set of projects for the expansion of employment does not seem to have existed at the beginning of the first Christian Democratic administration, there is reason for optimism based on the actual and potential availability of foreign exchange due to higher copper prices and the expansion of copper production, based on the rapid rise in manufacturing production which has already occurred, and based on the rhythm of plant openings and planned investments.

2. INCOME POLICY

It is in the area of income policy that we see the first signs of the dualism between the share going to labor as a whole vis-à-vis other sectors, on the one hand, and the policy of upgrading the poorest sectors within labor, on the other hand. Concerning the overall redistribution of income between wages and salaries and other sectors we have highly encouraging, but clearly inadequate, information. On the one hand, the "Memorandum on labor and social security policy" to which we have already referred[7] claims achievement of a "redistribution of national income in favor of the working sector to an extent hitherto

[7] "Memorandum sobre politica laboral y de seguridad social para el Congreso del Partido Democrata Cristiano," August 9, 1966, p. 5, Section II(d).

unknown in the history of Chile, indicating an increase in purchasing power of the salaried sector on the average of 10 percent with respect to the previous year." The paragraph goes on to state that "a principal part of this process has affected the peasant sector as a result of the upward leveling of their minimum wage to the minimum industrial wage."

As Table II shows, the share of national income going to salaries and wages did indeed increase substantially from 1964

TABLE II

PERCENT OF CHILE'S "GEOGRAPHIC NATIONAL INCOME"
BY TYPES OF INCOME, 1960–1966

	1 Income from Property or Entrepreneurship	2 Salary	3 Wages	4 Social Security	5 Total of Cols. 2–4
1960	52.9	20.8	19.6	6.7	47.1
1961	53.8	20.1	20.0	6.1	46.2
1962	53.7	20.5	19.5	6.3	46.3
1963	56.6	19.1	18.2	6.1	43.4
1964	56.2	18.7	19.1	6.0	43.8
1965	52.4	20.3	20.5	6.8	47.6
1966[1]	50.8	20.8	21.1	7.3	49.2

[1] Estimate.

Sources: Oficina de la Presidencia de la Republica (ODEPLAN). All figures based on previous figures of the Chilean Development Corporation (CORFO) and subject to revision.

to 1965, rising by about 4 percent from 43.8 to 47.6 percent, which is indeed almost a 10 percent increase on the basis of 43.8 = 100. The figure of 47.6 percent is not, however, substantially above the *Corporación de Fomento* (CORFO) figures for 1960 (47.1 percent), and might be attributed at least in part to the usual phenomenon that wages recuperate part of their purchasing power when inflation slows down (as it did in Chile in 1965) after a period of rapid inflation (in 1963 and 1964). However, the provisional figures for 1966 indicate a continuing

TABLE III

YEARLY INCREASE OF PRICES AND OF WAGES AND SALARIES, 1960–1966

	Consumer Price Index (Percentage increase of the average prices each year relative to average prices of previous years)	Wage and Salary Index (Percentage increase over previous year, April to April comparison)
1960	11.6	15.1
1961	7.7	15.1
1962	13.9	13.9
1963	44.3	36.3
1964	46.0	33.4
1965	28.8	54.0
1966	22.9	35.9

a. In 1965 and in 1966 wages rose by about the same as salaries. In 1964 salaries had risen much more than wages: 41 vs. 27 percent, though this may be due to taking April as basis for comparisons.

b. As between sectors, public utilities and mining have had increases relative to the common base period of April 1959 well above the average, while state employees (fiscales) and "semistate" employees (semifiscales) have had considerably less increase, the latter perhaps 20 percent less than the average.

Source: Published data of Dirección de Estadística y Censos.

increase in the share of national income going to labor, to reach a new high of 49.2 percent. If these figures should become definitive, and hold up under various statistical cross-analyses taking into account any possible rise in the proportion of the labor force earning salaries and wages, and so on, then the Frei government would indeed be justified in claiming success in its income redistribution policy. Present indications point in that direction.

A second way to measure the economic welfare of the working population is, of course, to examine what has happened to wage and salary rates in the past few years. Such an examination necessarily has two points of reference: average wage rates and earnings, on the one hand, and minimum wages—so important in Chile—on the other hand. In both cases the pace of inflation

TABLE IV

LEGAL MINIMUM WAGES AND SALARIES (IN ESCUDOS OF THE RESPECTIVE YEAR) FOR AGRICULTURAL AND INDUSTRIAL WORKERS (DAILY),[1] AND WHITE-COLLAR EMPLOYEES (MONTHLY),[1] BY YEAR

Year	Consumer Price Index (Increase over previous year)	Agricultural[2]		Industrial		White-Collar	
		$ pesos	% increase over previous year	$ pesos	% increase over previous year	$ pesos	% increase over previous year
1962	—	0.95	—	1.27	—	80.91	—
1963	44.3	1.35	42	1.62	28	103.32	28
1964	46.0	2.05	52	2.36	46	150.23	45
1965	28.8	3.26	59	[3]	38	207.92	38
1966	22.9	4.10	26		26	261.77	26

[1] To compare blue-collar with white-collar employees, the daily wage of the former could be multiplied by 30, since Sunday is paid if the previous six days were worked. This does assume a full work week, however. The industrial workers' wages will be found to be less than 50 percent of that of the white-collar employees.

[2] For the provinces of Valparaiso, Santiago, O'Higgins, and Colchagua. Other provinces, except for Magellanes, are lower.

[3] From mid-1965 onward, the agricultural minimum wage was raised to that of industrial workers (Law No. 16,464).

Source: Servicio de Seguro Social. Published in Boletín Mensual No. 466, December 1966 of the Banco Central de Chile.

must be taken into account, particularly since one of the stated goals of the Christian Democratic party was to slow down and ultimately to arrest the inflationary process.

As may be seen from Table III, the wage and salary index has during the last two years increased substantially more than the consumer price index. This is particularly notable in comparison with the years 1963 and 1964, when wage increases clearly lagged behind rises in the consumer price index.

Alternatively, as shown in Table IV, the problem of the purchasing power of wages and salaries may be approached by considering the legally established minima. While the situation presented in Table IV is not quite as dramatic as that in Table III, it is nevertheless clear that the government has indeed sought to achieve increases in legal minimum wages somewhat above increases in the consumer price index. The only temptation which, apparently, the government has not been able to resist is that of holding back the wages and salaries of those who most directly depend on it: its own employees. As mentioned in note (b) to Table III, state employees, and particularly that large group of employees known as semifiscales, still find their own salaries lagging far behind the index of wages and salaries which uses April 1959 as a base.

In general, however, it seems clear that the government has stood by its announced objective of favoring the wage and salary earner and helping to recover for him some of the purchasing power he lost during the inflation of the 1962–1964 period. The single most substantial raise in wages was given to the campesinos (peasants) in April 1965. Under Law No. 16,250 their minimum salary was made equal to that of industrial workers, which involved a rise of 59 percent. At the same time agricultural employers were no longer allowed to deduct housing as part of payment in kind; other payments in kind were made more secure, while the proportion which they could form of total wages paid was reduced; hours of work were better controlled; and a variety of other benefits was established. This particular favoritism toward one of the weakest groups in

Chilean society has been among the most significant subthemes of the government's general labor policy.

3. POWER VS. FREEDOM: THE REFORM OF THE LABOR CODE

The reform of Chile's labor code—which has not been modified substantially since it became a part of Chilean law in the mid-twenties[8]—has for many years been ardently desired not only by the Christian Democrats but by all parties of the Left. The many specific objections to the labor code raised by the Left could all be summarized under the single heading that the code weakened and limited the power of workers to deal with employers. Many Christian Democrats, on the other hand, for long have had not only that objection but a second one: that the code interfered with the right of workers to join unions of *their own choosing*. The Christian Democratic position is based only in part on an ideological commitment to the concept of freedom of choice, or on those streams of Catholic thought which, more in the past than today, have favored parallel unionism, that is, Catholic unions separate from unions dominated by Socialists and Communists. One of the strongest motives for supporting the concept of freedom of choice must rather be found in the personal and organizational frustrations of those Chilean trade unionists whose loyalties are not to the Socialist and Communist parties, but to other groups, including the Christian Democratic party.

Since Socialists and Communists, particularly when working in harmony, frequently command sufficient loyalty among union members to permit them to control union machinery, non-Marxists (and that may also include Radicals) find themselves systematically excluded from power and influence. This is particularly true at the level of the industrial federation

---

[8] For a most revealing history of the original code see James O. Morris, *Elites, Intellectuals, and Consensus: A Study of the Social Question and the Industrial Relations System in Chile* (Ithaca: New York State School of Industrial and Labor Relations, Cornell University, 1966).

("international" in United States terminology, that is, metal workers, miners, textile workers) and especially at the level of Chile's central labor body, Central Única de Trabajadores (CUT). In a study of local union presidents conducted in Chile in late 1962 and early 1963[9] it was notable that by far the largest group of presidents interviewed (43 percent) were loyal to either the Socialist or Communist parties, in comparison with 23 percent for Christian Democracy. The minority position of the Christian Democrats is aggravated by the fact that a far smaller percentage of the unions they control (38 percent) were affiliated with CUT than locals presided over by those loyal to FRAP, 68 percent of which were affiliated with CUT. Therefore, Christian Democrats and others who may speak for substantial sectors of labor, but who are yet a numerical minority with a weak organizational base, find themselves frustrated both at the local level (where unity is imposed by the present labor code which allows only one union per plant) and at higher levels, where rivals to CUT have not succeeded in challenging its supremacy.

For this reason much thought has been given within the Christian Democratic party to the dual problems of whether to establish organizations rivaling CUT and its industry federations and also whether to permit workers in the same plant to belong to different trade union locals. Opinions within the party differ on whether it would be to the ultimate benefit of the workers to have parallel movements. There is also disagreement about whether, from a purely practical point of view, rival movements would in fact be able to establish themselves against a Socialist and Communist opposition which would undoubtedly hurl the catchy accusation of "disrupting working class unity" against new contenders. And, finally, opinions differ on the question of whether the collective bargaining function of trade unions could be successfully managed from a purely

[9] Henry A. Landsberger, Manuel Barrera, and Abel Toro, "The Chilean Labor Union Leader: A Preliminary Report on His Background and Attitudes," Industrial and Labor Relations Review, XVII, 3 (April 1964), pp. 399–420.

administrative point of view. There is far less controversy, if any, over the general principle that groups of workers who differ from their Socialist and Communist leaders deserve the right to establish their own channels for expressing their wishes.

Nevertheless, these differences over tactics within the party have been sufficiently strong so that the bill presented to Congress on February 19, 1965, modifying various parts of the labor code dealing with union organization has not made progress, partly at the request of the party itself.[10] Naturally, the opposition to the bill on the part of the Radical party and of the National party (a fusion of the Liberal and Conservative parties) combined with the opposition of FRAP would have made the passage of this bill difficult if not impossible quite apart from lukewarmness on the part of PDC.

Unfortunately, disagreement over the advisability of permitting a minority within labor to organize formally has also held up the reform of other aspects of the present labor code on which there is actually very substantial agreement in PDC. These are the sections which now weaken a union relative to the employer (for example, by not providing for the legal recognition of federations as bargaining agents) and those sections which make a union highly dependent on the state both by giving the state an important discretionary role in the establishment of new unions and by intruding the state into the union's internal life, for example, the disbursement of funds. The bill introduced in 1965 would indeed make the establishment of unions administratively much easier and, above all, would give legal bargaining status to federations. All restrictions would be removed which prevent unions from financing their own administrative structure and which make any expenditure dependent on the countersignature of an inspector of labor. In addition, employers would find it more difficult to rid themselves of union officials by bribing them with the payment of high indemnities, and a long list of unfair employer labor practices would be

[10] "Memorandum sobre politica laboral . . ." p. 4, Section II(a).

established.[11] For industrial workers the only impressive legislative benefits obtained so far have been Laws No. 16,270 and 16,404, both approved in 1965, which make it more difficult to discharge workers, and Law No. 16,350, which increases from six to thirty the number of days of notice which have to be given prior to discharge.

Yet in the sections of the bill concerning internal union government we find that interesting undercurrent of concern with minority groups who may be excluded from the seats of power, a concern to which we have drawn attention at the beginning of this discussion. Very explicit mention is made of the right of union members personally to have access to the books of the union, and there is an explicit prohibition that any workers be subjected to pressure either to join or not to join a particular union. (Only members of the armed forces, the uniformed and civil police, and prison staffs are prohibited from forming unions.)

But the most substantial confirmation of our thesis that PDC is particularly concerned with raising the relative strength of the least privileged social sectors can be found in the fact that the bill modifying the current law on unionization of agricultural workers has been passed by Congress (with the help of the Socialist and Communist parties), signed by the President, and published on April 29, 1967. The new law (No. 16,625) might be summarized rather crudely by saying that the agricultural worker has now been given the same rights which the 1965 bill, still in Congress, envisions for industrial workers. Unions are no longer to be limited to a single farm (industrial plant in the case of urban labor). While the minimum number of members per union is raised from twenty-five, under the old law, to one hundred (even here Article 1 permits exceptions), members may now be drawn from any farm in the area. Massive protection is given to all candidates and holders of union offices (including, under Article 11, "shop stewards"), and Ministry

[11] Boletín No. 79, 1965, "Mensaje: Establece diversas normas sobre el derecho de asociación sindical," Cámara de Diputados, Comisión de Trabajo y Legislación Social.

of Labor surveillance of unions (for example, elections) is greatly reduced (Article 4), although as compared with the original bill, the power of the Ministry has clearly been increased, for example, in the matter of financial surveillance (Articles 15 and 16). Federations which negotiate on behalf of union members and their local unions may be established; employers must pay wages to officials for time spent on union business, and so on.

Both the new act (Article 14) and the bill covering urban workers make the payment of union dues obligatory for all members. Rural workers must pay in dues at least 2 percent of that part of their wage which is subject to social security (the union has the right to demand checkoff), and the employer must pay another 1 percent. Those who do not wish their dues to go to a union shall have them deposited in a special fund of the Ministry of Labor, part of which is to be used for worker education and training, the other part is to go to national federations in a manner to be established by administrative rules still to be formulated. The final sections of the bill dealing with collective bargaining, where the administrative problem has to be faced of how an employer whose workers may belong to different unions shall negotiate with any one of them, are rather general and put a good deal of power into the hands of the Ministry of Labor. Article 22 refers to administrative regulations under which the criterion and the procedure for determining the "organizations most representative of workers and of agricultural employers" shall be established, since it is only these "most representative" organizations which shall represent workers and which shall become members of certain mediation and conciliation commissions (Article 26).[12] It seems obvious that the administration of these sections of the law, whose intent seems to be to make sure that minority groups do not arrogate for themselves the right to speak for the majority, will prove difficult. A later section (Article 28 et seq.) for the first

[12] Diario Oficial No. 26730, April 29, 1967.

time recognizes the rural workers' right to strike. Once a strike is agreed upon in a secret, supervised vote by a majority of two-thirds of the membership, the employer cannot continue to work his farm except for work of "urgent necessity" which will be supervised by a labor inspector.

This law, while it still leaves a good deal to the discretion of the Ministry of Labor at crucial junctures, represents a massive advance in the trade union rights of rural workers. When viewed in conjunction with Law No. 16,250 of April 21, 1965, which makes the agricultural minimum wage equal to that of the industrial worker; with Law No. 16,455 of April 3, 1966, which establishes that even the casual agricultural laborer must be given thirty days' notice; and with Decree No. 202 of March 9, 1966, which establishes an eight-hour day and forty-eight-hour week for agricultural workers, it is clear that the Christian Democratic government has made a major effort to improve the lot of the agricultural worker. And this without even taking into account the new Agricultural Reform Law which was finally approved in mid-1967.

4. THE PRESENT UNION SITUATION

An interesting insight into how much can be done within an existing legal framework, provided the will is there, is revealed in that even in the absence of new legislation a very significant expansion of unionization has occurred in Chile. As it may be seen from Table V, the union movement in effect stagnated between 1944 and 1964 both in terms of numbers of unions and in terms of membership. During 1965, however, the total number of legally recognized unions increased by 175, or almost 10 percent, and in 1966 it increased by a massive 832 to a total of 2,870. Most interesting, of course, is the fact that the number of agricultural unions increased by over 600 percent, from 32 to 201, even under the old law. While Tables V and VI reveal that the increase in the number of unions was not matched by a completely proportional increase in the number of union

TABLE V

NUMBER AND PERCENT OF UNIONS, BY YEAR AND TYPE

Year	Industrial		Professional (Craft)		Agricultural		Total	
	No.	%	No.	%	No.	%	No.	%
1944	596	36	1,056	64	—	—	1,652	100
1954	677	33	1,372	66	19	1	2,068	100
1960	608	33	1,240	66	18	1	1,866	100
1961	618	35	1,124	64	22	1	1,764	100
1962	598	33	1,154	64	22	1	1,794	100
1963	656	35	1,174	63	22	2	1,852	100
1964	632	34	1,207	65	24	1	1,863	100
1965	687	34	1,319	65	32	2	2,038	100
1966	990	35	1,679	59	201	7	2,870	100

Source: Dirección del Trabajo, Departamento de Organizaciónes Sociales, Antecedentes Estadísticos del Departamento de Organizaciónes Sociales, 1960-1965.
For 1944 and 1954 see Appendix "D," Boletín No. 79, "Mensaje: Establece diversas normas sobre el derecho de asociación sindical," Cámara de Diputados.

TABLE VI

NUMBER AND PERCENT OF UNION MEMBERS, BY YEAR AND TYPE OF UNION

Year	Industrial		Professional (Craft)		Agricultural		Total	
	No.	%	No.	%	No.	%	No.	%
1944	143,860	58	103,221	42	—	—	247,081	100
1954	165,888	56	132,161	44	1,315	0	299,364	100
1960	122,306	53	106,326	46	1,424	1	230,129	100
1961	144,650	56	111,082	43	1,831	1	257,563	100
1962	134,478	54	110,669	45	1,860	1	247,007	100
1963	143,912	55	117,086	45	1,500	1	262,498	100
1964	142,958	53	125,926	47	1,658	1	270,542	100
1965	154,561	53	135,974	47	2,118	1	292,653	100
1966	179,506	51	161,363	46	10,647	3	352,516	100

To this might be added employees in the public sector. Excluding the Ministry of Defense, Carabineros, and Investigaciónes, there were about 234,000 such employees in 1962. Perhaps another 74,600 persons listed as "directors, professionals, and technicians" should also be excluded as not unionized, though this is more doubtful. (Source of these figures is Eunice Riquelme de Díaz, Recursos humanos de la Administración Publica Chilena, [Santiago, Chile: INSORA, Faculty of Economic Sciences, University of Chile, 1963].) Accepting the figure of 234,000 as a maximum, we find seventeen federations covering 124,500 of these individuals according to Jorge Barria, Trayectoria y estructura del Movimiento Sindical Chileno (Santiago, Chile: INSORA, 1963), or well over 50 percent. For various reasons this is a minimum figure.

Source: Dirección del Trabajo, Departamento de Organizaciónes Sociales, Antecedentes Estadísticos del Departamento de Organizaciónes Sociales, 1960–1965.

members, so that there was a consequent decline in the average number of members per union (see Table VII), the fact nevertheless remains that total union membership increased between 1965 and 1966 by the very substantial figure of sixty thousand, or more than 20 percent. Some observers have attributed this decline in average membership per union to the divisive tactics of the Christian Democrats. But a far more probable explanation is that as unionization proceeds, it must necessarily concern itself with smaller plants, since it is likely that larger plants were organized long ago. This explanation is all the more plausible since under the present law no "atomization" of existing unions is legally possible.

TABLE VII

AVERAGE NUMBER OF MEMBERS PER UNION, BY YEAR AND TYPE

Year	Industrial	Professional (Crafts)	Agricultural	Total
1944	241	98	—	150
1954	156	96	69	145
1963	219	99	66	142
1964	226	104	69	145
1965	225	103	66	144
1966	181	96	53	123

Source: Dirección del Trabajo, Departamento de Organizaciónes Sociales, Antecedentes Estadísticos del Departamento de Organizaciónes Sociales, 1960–1965.

Finally, it should be noted that official figures probably underestimate the extent to which unionization has increased in Chile during the past few years, since these figures include only legally established unions. In the agricultural sector in particular a vast number of de facto unions now exist which simply have not bothered to seek official recognition. The advantages of recognition were, under the old law, practically nil since the most important activity of the union, the presentation of con-

TABLE VIII

NUMBER OF LEGAL AND ILLEGAL STRIKES AND CONTRACT
DEMANDS (PLIEGOS), BY YEAR

Year	1 Legal Strikes	2 Illegal Strikes	3 Total Strikes	4 Total Pliegos	5 % of Strikes to Pliegos
1959	10	197	207	1,134	18.2
1960	85	160	245	1,608	15.2
1961	82	180	262	1,678	15.6
1962	85	316	401	1,282	31.2
1963	50	366	416	1,495	27.8
1964	88	476	564	1,939	29.1
1965	148	575	723	2,931	24.6
1966	137	936	1,073	NA*	NA*

* NA = not available at the time of writing.
Source: Dirección del Trabajo, Departamento de Conflictos Colectivos, Sueldos
y Salarios.

TABLE IX

NUMBER OF MAN-DAYS LOST THROUGH STRIKES (LEGAL AND ILLEGAL),
BY YEAR AND TYPE OF WORKER

Year	Blue-Collar (Obrero)		White-Collar (Empleado)		Total	
	No. Strikes	Days Lost	No. Strikes	Days Lost	No. Strikes	Days Lost
1962	258	795,055	51	37,332	309	832,387
1963	351	728,362	61	57,395	412	785,757
1964	464	773,791	128	61,393	592	835,184
1965	787	1,686,775	109	215,103	896	1,901,878

Source: Dirección del Trabajo, Departamento de Conflictos.

tract demands, could legally be performed by groups of workers
not formally joined together in a recognized union. It has been
estimated that the number of functioning agricultural unions

may be double, triple, or quadruple the two hundred officially recognized.

Strikes. Tables VIII and IX show that there has been a very substantial rise in both the number of strikes and in days lost through strikes. The evidence is quite clear: industrial conflict, already on the rise between 1963 and 1964, increased precipitously between 1964 and 1965. The number of days lost through both legal and illegal strikes more than doubled, while the number of strikes increased by 50 percent, which indicates that at least some of the strikes were long. Detailed figures by province show that Tarapacá and Antofagasta (the mining regions), Santiago and Valparaíso, and finally Concepción, were the areas in which massive increases in strike activity occurred; in many other provinces the number of days lost through strikes actually decreased. We know that there were massive and repeated strikes in the copper and banking industries.

At this distance from the situation it is of course impossible to know the causes of such an increase in strike activity. While politics—the antagonism of Radical, Socialist, and Communist trade union leaders toward the government—undoubtedly has played some part in the picture, it is unlikely that "politics" was more than one cause of the unrest, and its role should not be exaggerated. The fact that the average Chilean worker will not blindly follow his leaders, and will not strike unless he feels his own interests are affected, was after all once again brought out after the tragic shooting of striking miners at "El Salvador" in mid-1966, when a protest strike called by CUT failed to materialize. Few labor movements—or any other economic interest groups—have ever been known for overdoses of social responsibility, as the restlessness of United States labor even during the critical war years, and the restlessness of British unions even under friendly labor governments, should make apparent. It is doubtful that the Chilean worker, or even his leader, is significantly different from his counterparts in the countries just cited. Restlessness is probably—and ironically—due substantially to the prosperity and optimism which the

Christian Democratic government is creating: the feeling that it should be possible to squeeze something out of a friendly government where an unfriendly one would turn a cold shoulder.

5. OTHER PROJECTS TO INCREASE SOCIAL WELFARE

It is the thesis of this article that a fundamental characteristic of the Christian Democratic program, both for idealistic and for practical political reasons, is to help and to organize those sectors of the underprivileged which are in even worse condition than organized labor, and to do so directly, thereby in part bypassing an organized labor movement which is substantially in the hands of the opposition. There is not space to present detailed information on the housing, education, and health programs of the government or on *Promoción Popular*. Yet these programs should be regarded as a most important facet of the Christian Democratic party's labor effort in the broad sense. The following facts, taken from the speech which President Frei made on the occasion of the second anniversary of his government,[13] will indicate the stress on social welfare projects under the Christian Democrats.

Concerning *education*, President Frei stated that in two years 9,811 new classrooms had been constructed with a total floor space of 1,100,000 square meters, which compares favorably with the construction of 1,000,000 square meters in the six preceding years when school construction had by no means been neglected. There were, at the end of 1966, 200,000 more children in school than in 1964, and compulsory education had been increased from six to eight years. In addition, 7,000 new teachers had been hired. More recent information indicates that in 1966, 2,300,000 children attended primary, secondary, and

---

[13] "Discurso del Presidente Frei con motivo de celebrar el segundo aniversario de su gobierno, en presencia de dirigentes y miembros del Partido Democrata Cristiano, en el Teatro Caupolican," Presidencia de la Republica, Secretaria de Prensa, November 4, 1966. (Third State of the Nation Address by President Eduardo Frei to the Joint Series of Congress, May 21, 1967.)

technical schools as compared with 1,800,000 in 1964, an increase of half a million, or about 33 percent.

A particular source of pride was the newly established *Instituto Nacional de Capacitación Profesional* (INACAP) for the training of skilled workers. During the election President Frei had spoken of establishing a "university of labor," of which INACAP is considered to be a part. It trained more than 20,000 persons in the first ten months of 1966 and planned to give skill training to 31,000 more in 1967. The possibility of raising blue-collar minimum wages to the same level as white-collar minimum wages is seen as depending on raising the skill level of blue-collar workers.

In the area of *health*, President Frei referred briefly to the fact that two thousand new employees had been added to the National Health Service and that this had permitted the number of medical consultations to rise from 7,800,000 per year to over 10,000,000 in 1966. Finally, President Frei could point "with pride" to the construction of 86,000 *housing units* in the first two years of his regime, which came relatively close to the 95,000 which had been promised and fell short only because the quota assigned to the copper industry had not been fulfilled. The establishment of a new Ministry of Housing, of course, also gives some indication of the seriousness with which this part of the program is being regarded.

Most revolutionary, however, at least in potential and conception, has been the *Promoción Popular* program. It envisages the legal recognition of neighborhood centers, mothers' clubs, sports clubs, and so on, especially in the poorer areas. It would endow them with some of the privileges, power, and means of local government units, not so much subordinate to, as parallel to, existing municipal authorities and subject to a certain amount of guidance from a specially established ministry of the central government. This project, sent to Congress in February, 1966, has, of course, run into considerable opposition from both the Right and Left, strongly entrenched as they are in the existing local authority structure. The bill has made little progress; it is clearly too novel and threatening a measure.

6. Some Interesting Partial Failures

The three most important areas in which little advance seems to have occurred are all in the legislative field, obviously due in large part to the fact that the Christian Democrats do not control Congress. The first failure we have already referred to and will discuss no further: the failure to reform the labor code in its entirety. The second failure concerns the reform of the social security system, and the third, the so-called "reform of the enterprise." The cause of these failures is uncertain. But it is reasonable to suppose that, apart from legislative congestion in Congress, reform of the social security system has so far been impossible at least in part because of the opposition of a number of vested interests, not so much on the part of employers, as on that of some employee groups who are presently particularly favored. But two important, though partial attempts, to bring some order into the Chilean social security system have nevertheless been made with the introduction into Congress in December 1965 of a bill concerning family services and another dealing with accident insurance.

While the bill dealing with family services was still in its first constitutional step in the lower house in April 1967, it is worth summarizing briefly because its drafting reveals a good deal of political skill, as well as some of the philosophical underpinings of the government's thinking.

Notable, for example, is the fact that the government intends to make a start, in this particular area of family allowances and services, with the very ticklish task of eliminating the differences in benefits given to blue-collar as compared with white-collar workers,[14] almost invariably to the detriment of the former, of course. This morally unjustifiable and socially distasteful distinction has long been deplored in Chile, but no one has dared to do anything about it. The fact that the Christian Democratic government is willing to grasp this nettle is a sign

[14] See page 6 of the "Memorandum sobre politica laboral . . ." which accompanied the bill sent to Congress, as well as Articles 20 and 21 of the "Proyecto" (bill) itself.

of its courage, its belief in rationality, and a further example of the PDC's policy of favoring the "least favored among the less favored." The inclusion of independent workers—an immense step forward—is also a sign of concern for some of the poorest sectors of society.

The political skill inherent in the bill to which we referred above consists in making explicit that uniformity in family allowances will not bring with it the administrative dissolution of the dozens of separate social security institutions which currently disburse these allowances. The threat of such administrative rationalization, and the elimination of jobs it implies, would have been too much to swallow. Indeed, the bill encourages the establishment on the basis of profession or geographic region of new administrative units at the discretion of the President, and justifies this both on the basis that European experience has shown that overly large as well as overly small institutions have high administrative costs, and on the more ideological basis that institutions intermediate between the citizen and the state and administered by the citizens are in themselves desirable. The latter philosophy obviously goes back to the papal social encyclicals and the "principle of subsidiarity."[15] The influence of the encyclicals may also account for the emphasis in the message accompanying the bill that monetary allowances are only one part of the services with which it is expected to provide the family. Family education and social services of various kinds are expected to be an integral part of the total concept of a *Sistema Nacional de Prestaciónes Familiares*[16] designed to strengthen the family as an institution and its dedication to the education of its children (the bill envisages the highest rate of allowances for older children attending educational institutions).

The bill dealing with accident insurance can be more briefly

[15] See, for example, *Mater et Magistra*, Part II, para. 53, where *Quadragesimo anno* is cited with approval on this point. (*Seven Great Encyclicals* [Glen Rock, New Jersey: Paulist Press], p. 230.)

[16] See pages 1 and 5 of the "Memorandum sobre politica laboral . . .," and Article 24, which, however, leaves specifics to administrative regulations to be issued in the future.

reviewed. It takes the big step forward of making it obligatory on an employer to insure his workers and makes both premiums and benefits independent of risk. But as in the case of family allowances it specifically does not set up a single, centralized system, but rather envisages the setting up of separate funds for different industries, to be administered by organizations administering other social services (for example, family allowances) for that industry. Indeed, envisaged is the dissolution of the existing *Caja* which is open to all employers of blue-collar workers who cannot or do not want to take out insurance policies with private insurance companies. The message accompanying the bill is notable (as is that dealing with family services) for its detailed references to the experience of other countries and for its general tone of intense humanitarianism. One suspects that the knowledgeable pen of the Minister of Labor, William Thayer A., had a role in their writing.

The third major legislative failure has been the absence of progress on the so-called "reform of the enterprise," no doubt both because of opposition from employers and because, however laudable and idealistic the aspiration, schemes are not at hand which are administratively viable and which actually fulfill the purpose of involving the mass of workers in the management of the enterprise. Neither German nor French experience has proved that various methods of joint consultation, codetermination, and shared planning have the kind of psychological impact on the worker which was initially expected; and, presumably, Chileans concerned with such problems are becoming rapidly aware of that fact as they study these experiences prior to drafting their own law. Interestingly enough, however, one of the reasons given by the Chilean government for the failure to install a system of industrial democracy is that it would be futile to do so given the existing structure of the union movement, which is "antidemocratic, anti-Frei, anti-Christian Democrat, and determined on the failure of the Revolution in Freedom in all those vital centers which are controlled by Marxism and the counterrevolution."[17]

[17] "Memorandum sobre politica laboral . . .," p. 11, Section IV(a).

It should be also noted that reform of the internal machinery of the Ministry of Labor, which has so frequently been claimed essential, had not yet taken place by April 1967. Its salary scale in particular has not yet been improved. Nevertheless, one or two extremely important administrative reforms have been put into practice. To deal with the shortage of permanent labor inspectors, for example, Law No. 16,464 authorized the Ministry to invest certain government officials with the authority of *ad hoc* work inspectors. Moreover, regulations concerning the fining of employers for infractions of the labor law have been strengthened. It is quite possible that relatively minor administrative modifications of this kind could, if enforced, be of more benefit to the underprivileged than the attempt to pass many a piece of major legislation.

No one reviewing the activities of the Christian Democratic government to date, evaluating both what it has tried to do and what it has actually been able to do, can accuse it of being inactive or untrue to its word. In many ways, of course, the Christian Democratic government's humane attitude toward the underprivileged is not startlingly new. It is rather the dramatic heightening of a theme which has been heard in Chile, sometimes loudly and sometimes softly, for many decades. Chile was one of the first countries to pass comprehensive labor legislation. Chilean managers were among the first, after World War II, to accept institutions which could help them to become more professional in their work: Chilean Institute for the Rational Administration of Enterprises (ICARE) and the *Servicio de Cooperación Técnica* are symbols of such an approach.[18] Moreover, studies of the attitudes of Chilean management in general[19] and

---

[18] Frederick Harbison and Charles E. Myers, *Management in the Industrial World: International Analysis* (New York: McGraw-Hill, 1959), Ch. 9, pp. 169–184.

[19] Guillermo Briones, *El empresario industrial en America Latma: 3. Chile* (United Nations Economic and Social Council, E/CN.12/642/Add.3, February 10, 1963), p. 50, see esp. p. 37 *et seq.*

of personnel managers in particular[20] have all indicated that management in Chile is more flexible toward labor than one might expect in a developing country. To this extent the Christian Democratic party is continuing a great tradition.

Nevertheless, it is also clear that the high intelligence, the ideals, energy, and political acumen, of the men at the helm of the party and of the Chilean state are responsible for the very substantial progress which labor has made in the first two years of the Christian Democratic regime. It is a record that is unsurpassed, and probably even unequaled, in benefiting the underprivileged as a whole, and the least privileged most of all.

[20] Henry A. Landsberger and Raul Dastres, *La situación y el pensamiento del administrador de personal chileno* (Santiago, Chile: INSORA, Faculty of Economic Sciences, University of Chile, 1963), p. 52, see esp. p. 33 *et seq.*

Part IV:
Political Aspects

8: IDEOLOGY OF POLITICAL DEVELOPMENT

Mario Artaza

In a recent publication of The Foreign Policy Association an analysis is made of the present political situation of Chile, and after a brief description of the ideological postulates of Christian Democracy the writer concludes that "to practical-minded Americans, such ideological formulations may seem tedious and irrelevant to the real social needs of a nation."[1]

Any document issued by the Christian Democratic party (PDC) is immediately distinguished by its constant references to an ideology. For example, in the final declaration of its last congress held in September 1966 the Revolution in Freedom is defined as "the step of the capitalistic society to the communitarian society," and the proclamation is made that "its historic aim is to achieve such a society." "This objective," continues the declaration, "begins with the present social and economic reality and through a revolutionary process goes on to establish the bases of a new society. This process is expressed and nourished around an ideology, and is based fundamentally on the action of the social forces held in check by the existing system."[2]

For the current European or American observer, and also for the scholar, this kind of statement is received with surprise and at times with concern. At other times it may be considered as mere verbal clothing intended to give conceptual elevation to pragmatic measures. Always a doubt spontaneously arises regarding the necessity or the appropriateness when a party with the

[1] "Christian Democracy in Action." Great Decisions 1967 (The Foreign Policy Association), p. 65.
[2] "Documentos," Política y Espíritu (October 1966), 66.

149

responsibilities of government shows a high concern for the ideological factors that should govern its action.

A search for a reply to these interrogations brings us directly to the field of political development, in which different sciences —politics, economics, and sociology—in efforts at times similar and other times contradictory, are only just beginning to penetrate cautiously.

Silvert has defined political development as a facet of "total development" which presupposes "the existence of a truly national community and of a government which can order social and economic relationships in such a way as to foster economic efficiency and social mobility. The nation-state gives political definition to the national community within which general development takes place."[3]

How does one estimate this type of development? In the patient elaboration of theories, more or less solid, on political development scholars have a favorite tool of which they make frequent use: the comparative study of existing political systems. This study almost always requires a model that exhibits certain characteristics, in this case the modern society of the Western world. The step that follows is the building of graduated tables in which the various levels are assigned through the use of indicators that translate the degree of expression of the characteristics existing in the model, which logically occupies the highest level.

In establishing these models the political scientist keeps in mind that the history of the West may be synthesized in the battle of centuries that culminates in the formation of nation-states. That is why the concepts of modernization and of nation-building sometimes turn out to be joined or confused with one another.

From the analysis of these models have sprung innumerable indicators of development of a socioeconomic nature, from which it may be deduced that political development is in some

[3] K. H. Silvert, Chile—Yesterday and Today (New York: Holt, Rinehart and Winston, 1965) p. 190.

way or another indissolubly tied in with socioeconomic development. The forms that are assumed by this interdependence and
its mechanisms of operation have resisted, up to now, efforts of
systematization, and continue to present surprises to every initiate. In a provocative article by Alfred Stepan an effort is made
to demonstrate that the experience of Latin America offers very
interesting peculiarities insofar as they refer to the relationship
between socioeconomic change and the creation of new values
and political patterns associated with modernity.[4] According to
Stepan, and he gives some examples, the mere growth of an
indicator of development does not have to lead inevitably to
political development. On the other hand, a series of impon-
derables may come to have such importance in political development that the use of more sophisticated indicators would
only yield results of secondary relevance.

As Professor Charles Anderson has stated it, the problem of
political development may be approached from two different
angles. One would bring us to the study of the capacity and
effectiveness of a government to face up to the demands of a
rapid economic growth. The other would force us to go deeply
into the study of political theory per se.[5]

The first angle, fundamentally instrumentalist, is basically
wise if we consider that the goal of politics is the attainment of
the common good, which today presupposes socioeconomic
development. As Anderson indicates, "Modern 'structuralist'
approaches to the economic development of Latin America . . .
direct the bulk of their recommendations to public authorities.
It is the state's responsibility to stimulate major changes in the
structure of economic institutions. . . ."[6] The factor of the
capacity of public powers to influence the process of develop-

---

[4] Alfred Stepan, "Political Development Theory: The Latin American Experience," Journal of International Affairs, XX, 2 (1966), 223 ff.
[5] Charles W. Anderson, "Political Factors in Latin American Economic Development," Journal of International Affairs, XX, 2 (1966), 235 ff.
[6] Ibid., 237.

ment was brought out very clearly by John XXIII in *Mater et Magistra*.[7]

The second angle translates the development of concepts such as person, state, freedom and its reciprocal relations, and the use of power in a determined society. Logically, to secure a total perspective of political development the two angles must be used. The definition of Silvert, quoted at the beginning, presupposed both angles. To obtain "a truly national community" a study of the capacity of the state element to fulfill this primary objective is required. On the other hand, only the development of a comprehensive and realistic political theory can give us the key to a national community.

According to Matossian, "Ideology may be defined as a pattern of ideas which simultaneously provides for its adherents: a) a self-definition, b) a description of the current situation, its background and what is likely to follow, and c) various imperatives which are "deduced" from the foregoing."[8]

The concept of "ideology" is not yet found sufficiently refined and with respect to development is used without greater precision. Thus, from the sociological point of view Irving Louis Horowitz has carried out interesting studies on the contraposition of ideological policies with respect to mere "ideologies of development."[9] Silvert, from a definition of social values as a point of departure, considers that these "become manageable in conscious ways when they are translated into ideologies." Chileans are divided between those "who have a traditional set of values and ideologies, and those who hold modern views." And he adds that "This struggle between the politics of custom [those adhering to traditional values] and the politics of rationality [those desiring modernization] is the key to an understanding of ideological differences in Chile."[10]

[7] *Mater et Magistra*, Part II, para. 54.

[8] Matossian, "Ideologies of Delayed Industrialization: Some Tensions and Ambiguities," in John Kautsky, ed., *Political Change in Underdeveloped Countries* (New York: John Wiley & Sons, 1962), p. 253.

[9] Irving Louis Horowitz, *Three Worlds of Development* (New York: Oxford University Press, 1966), pp. 60–61 and 239–240.

[10] Silvert, *op. cit.*, p. 115.

The use of models and of an indicator of development has created a strong tendency among many political scientists to adopt a pragmatic and determinist position with respect to political development. This leads to a relegation to second place of the study of the role that ideology must play in the process. Even more, the use of the word "ideology" has come to have a certain derogatory connotation.

This is understandable if we consider the secondary role of ideology in the political life of a majority of the developed nations of the West. This is due, in great measure, to the fact that ideological goals have already been attained, or what is more frequent, what is ideal in most of the developing countries is found in them converted into reality as a living fact. Therefore, policy in the more advanced countries develops mainly on a pragmatic plane. To obtain power in the United States or France means a completely different thing from obtaining power in Chile, for example. And this for the simple reason that in the first case only small variations are needed in existing structures for the common good, while in the second an intensive revolutionary process is required to gain the same goal.

When as yet a high level of development has not been reached, it is urgent to have a philosophical basis to confront politics. As Eduardo Frei has said, "the state, society, education and family are results of ideas that political parties inspire in man and in the social body."[11]

By using the conceptual table of political development that the two angles offer us, it is easy to discover why the Christian Democratic party insists on the necessity of constructing an ideological foundation for successfully carrying out a process of change and development. In fact, judgment on the quality of the state instrument in Chile and the ineffectiveness of its action with respect to the problems of underdevelopment indicated that it was necessary to achieve a true revolution to make it adequate to the necessities of the times. On the other hand,

---

[11] Eduardo Frei, *Religion, Revolution and Reform* (New York: Praeger, 1964), p. 36.

this judgment on the inefficiency of the state instrument was based not only on practical reasons, in a mere desire for modernization, but on values determined by a different concept of the state, in which the massive participation of the people in the political process, in culture, and in wealth was assured.

Thus, it is very difficult to find in history the case of a revolution (which has been defined as a swift and radical change, deliberately produced, of existing structures) that has not been inspired by a "force-idea," by a theoretical justification, in short, by an ideology. Therefore, it is completely rational and legitimate to introduce the concept of ideology as an integral element of the definition of revolution.

Every movement springs from an animating vision. It is always the thought that illuminates action. In order to carry out a revolution, a vision of the future is necessary from which are deduced the values that must serve, as Claudio Orrego said in Chile,[12] as the "measuring stick of the existing situation that is repudiated." That is, it is the values of the future which serve to measure present reality.

Without a system of ideas it is impossible to reach an understanding of a human community or the meaning of the exercise and the aim of power. Without an ideology it is difficult for a political order to come into being. As it was eloquently stated in the prologue to a work of Eduardo Frei, which suggestively bears the title Thought and Action, it is impossible to enunciate and apply a coherent policy if a central thought, an organic vision of man and of society, does not inspire it.[13]

For a Latin American, a being that still seeks to define his yet nebulous identity, ideology is indispensable if he aspires to undertake a revolutionary process, which nobody denies to be necessary. Hence the attraction and the success of Communism, which offers an apparently integral answer to all man's

[12] Claudio Orrego Vicuña, "Esquema para una comprensión objetiva de la Revolución en Libertad," Política y espíritu (November-December 1966), 62.

[13] Eduardo Frei, Pensamiento y acción (Santiago de Chile: Ed. del Pacífico, 1956), Prologue, p. 13.

aspirations. And hence the necessity of presenting a profound theoretical plan, such as that offered by the Christian Democrats in Chile, supporting a concrete revolutionary program.

In every scheme of a revolutionary process, ideology has a role to play. Claudio Orrego, in describing what he calls "mechanisms of a policy of changes," indicates that every revolutionary attempt implies the presence of closely linked elements: (1) an ideological project (a communitarian society in the case of the Christian Democrats of Chile), (2) a historical situation which it is necessary to account for and that in an important manner conditions the possibility of faithfully carrying out the ideological project, and (3) a political will that is capable of giving impulse to a program in accordance with the synthesis that may be possible between the elements indicated in (1) and (2). Orrego adds that it is then necessary to choose the means of action and make the indispensable evaluation of costs (possible sacrifices), and to divide, finally, the revolutionary process in stages, each with its own political strategy. In each stage a program should be adopted within the total ideological context.[14]

With this in mind it is pertinent for us to formulate the following questions with respect to the political development of Chile:

1. Given the historical evolution of Chile, was it essential to advance the necessity of revolutionary changes?

2. Of what does the ideology that is directing this revolutionary process consist and what specific measures has it proposed?

According to Radomiro Tomić,[15] in order to put into practice a revolutionary project the presence of the following factors is necessary. First, a revolutionary situation of an objective character. Revolutions are not invented or created out of thin air. They break forth from irresistible tensions between the various social groups that compose a community and the institutions that give expression to a type of social order. Second, a revolutionary theory (ideology). Third, the presence of revolution-

---

[14] Orrego, op. cit., pp. 63–64.
[15] From conversations with the author, January and February 1967.

aries, the leaders or catalyzers of the tensions whose basic task is to promote the transfer of power within ideological channels.

According to Tomić, the major revolutionary task is that of transferring to the national majorities the responsibility of the generation of political power, access to education at all levels, and access to wealth. This transference of the exercise of political power to the majorities should assure the attainment of the common good.

These factors become operative in such measure as the following elements exist in a country:

1. A people conscious of the situation of the political, economic, and social underdevelopment in which they exist, and mobilized with real and lofty motives.

2. A generous and dynamic youth, with a consciousness of the role it is called upon to play in the promotion of the idea of a practice of solidarity.

3. Intellectuals ready to direct the process of change and capable of creating the programmatic conditions necessary for attaining the ideological goals.

4. Popular consensus with respect to the need for change and the goals and proposed ways for attaining them.

Tomić added two additional elements necessary for this revolution to be able to take place within the framework of democracy. First, that minorities remain loyal to the basic rules of the give-and-take of democracy and do not attempt to arrest by violent means or dilatory, arbitrary procedures the access of the majority to control of the effective means of political, social, and economic power. Second, a favorable international situation that permits the development of a revolutionary process without domestic efforts having to be sacrificed because of external security reasons and, on the other hand, that assures an adequate level of external solidarity.

According to PDC, during the last presidential elections in Chile there existed in that country "an objective revolutionary situation." Therefore, the PDC emphasized that the triumph of its candidate, Eduardo Frei, would open the way to a Revolution in Freedom. Of what did this objective revolutionary situation consist?

For many the mere mention of this question in connection with Chile has seemed very strange. Chile could take pride in more that 130 years of political stability, broken only by scarcely 4 years of irregular government. The Constitution of 1833 remained in effect until 1925, and the one adopted that year has continued to be respected faithfully by successive executives, legally elected, together with senators, representatives, and municipal regimes. The judicial power is properly constituted and independent. The armed forces traditionally respect the Constitution and the law. The population is homogeneous, and there is no racial problem. In high measure Chileans have a sense of nationality, of belonging, and of national solidarity. For dispassionate observers, such as Professors K. H. Silvert and Frederick Pike, Chile possesses a long list of attributes indicative of a high level of political maturity.[16]

Ernst Halperin has written that "Chile's record of political stability is excellent by Latin American and good by even European standards. In the more than one hundred and thirty years that have passed since the consolidation of the Chilean state it has seen less civil strife and revolution than France, Germany or Italy."[17]

This stability indicated to the superficial observer the presence of elements of political development of sufficient importance to conclude that Chile had achieved or was on the way to achieving the necessary adaptations of its economic and social structure by means of a peaceful evolution, like the nations of Western Europe.

But behind this institutional stability, of which the Chilean may certainly be proud and which has served to create undeniably democratic values and principles, there existed a socio-

[16] Silvert, op. cit., p. 191; Pike, Chile and the United States: 1880–1962 (Notre Dame: University of Notre Dame Press, 1963), Introduction, p. xx.

[17] Ernst Halperin, Nationalism and Communism in Chile (Cambridge, Mass.: The M.I.T. Press, 1965), pp. 2–27.

economic reality that was not at the level for which its political evaluation gave hope.

Very briefly there are set down here the elements of this socioeconomic situation that marked an objectively revolutionary situation.

1. OF AN ECONOMIC CHARACTER

(a) *Insufficient dynamism in economic development.* Between 1940 and 1963 the rate of growth of per-capita income was 1.5 percent annually accumulative. With this rate of growth forty-five years were required to double the present per-capita income,[18] which is less than U.S.$450.

(b) *Unjust distribution of income.* In 1964, 37 percent of Chilean families participated in 8 percent of the total income of the country.[19] In an economically active population of 2.4 million (20 percent women), 1.8 million received 25 percent of the national income; 360,000 received another 25 percent; and, at the other extreme, only 220,000 persons, or 9 percent, received 50 percent of the national income.[20] The Chilean economist Jorge Ahumada was able to say that Chile presented "the spectacle of the sordid poverty of the masses in contrast to the proud ostentation of the minority."[21]

(c) *Chronic inflation and devaluation of the currency.* In the 1940's prices increased at an annual rate of 17.7 percent. In the fifties the annual rate was 38 percent. After a brief period of restrained inflation in 1960 and 1961, during the years 1963 and 1964 it reached an annual average of 42 percent. Between 1945 and 1964 the price of the dollar rose from 32 pesos to 3,200 pesos.[22]

(d) *Situation of agriculture.* The income of the farmworkers,

---

[18] President Frei, State of the Nation Address (May 21, 1965), p. 5.
[19] *Ibid.*
[20] DESAL, *Encuesta sobre Chile* (1962), p. 57.
[21] Jorge Ahumada, *En vez de la miseria* (Santiago, Chile: Ed del Pacífico, 1958), p. 12.
[22] President Frei, State of the Nation Address, p. 6.

who comprise 92.1 percent of the agricultural sector of the country, was only 34 percent of the total, while the entrepreneurial sector, 7.6 percent of the population, received 65.6 percent of the income.[23] While the population of Chile increases at the rate of 2.26 percent per year, agricultural production has increased over the past twenty years at the rate of less than 2 percent. This has made necessary an increasing importation of foodstuffs by the government. According to the census of 1955 there are 151,000 farms in Chile. 76,000 has less than ten hectares in area. Within this total, more than 28,000 contained less than one hectare (2.47 acres). But there were 6,326 farms, or 4 percent of the total, that embraced 81 percent of the land.

1. OF A SOCIOCULTURAL CHARACTER

(a) *Deficient educational system.* The average schooling of those more than 15 years of age was 4 years in the urban sector and 2.5 years in the rural sector. School dropouts were such that only thirty-four of each one hundred children that entered elementary school completed the six years of this section.[24] There was a lack of schools and teachers, which is why thousands of children remained outside the educational system each year. In secondary education the situation was no better. For each one hundred students beginning in high school, only twenty-four completed the course. At the University of Chile only 2 percent of the students came from families of workers.

(b) *Housing deficit.* The First National Housing Census, taken in 1955, revealed that 30 percent of the population lived in houses that did not meet minimum health standards. In 1959 it was estimated that Chile needed urgently to build more than 500,000 housing units.

(c) *Nutrition deficiency.* Chile, with an average diet of 2,330 calories daily and 70 grams of proteins per person, belonged, according to Josué de Castro, in the category of countries in

---

[23] CIDA, *Study of Land Tenure in Chile* (1966), p. 28.
[24] President Frei, State of the Nation Address, p. 68.

which there existed "extremely defective alimentation, in which quantitative hunger is combined with qualitative insufficiencies of diet."[25]

(d) *Disease and infant mortality.* Life expectancy at birth in Chile is fifty years for men and fifty-four for women. The rate of infant mortality in 1959 was 117.2 per thousand.[26]

This picture, filled with obscure clouds of torment, is darkened even more if other factors are considered. The economic and social situation of the farmworker provoked, as an inexorable consequence, an increasing exodus toward the cities. From 1940 to 1950 more than 400,000 people migrated from the countryside to the cities, and from 1950 to 1960, more than 550,000.[27] These people, due to their lack of technical training, obtained only low-paying jobs, generally nonproductive ones. An analysis of the social situation revealed that "vast sectors of the population did not participate directly in Chilean society." That is to say, "a situation of marginality was shown as a consequence of a process of social disintegration."[28]

How did this deplorable socioeconomic situation reflect on the political development of Chile? The stability of its political system has not failed to impress observers. A serious study of political systems in developing countries placed Chile at a very high level for its degree of competitiveness and political modernity.[29]

For Halperin, "The stability of the democratic regime of Chile is to be attributed not to economic and sociological factors but to something so completely intangible as mere tradition."[30] Democracy of the nineteenth century, although aristocratic and with very restricted suffrage, sufficed to establish a

[25] Josué de Castro, "Geopolitics of Hunger," *Mensaje*, 123 (October 1963).
[26] *Ibid.*
[27] Message that accompanied the Agrarian Reform Project, p. 11.
[28] Amalio Fiallio, *Criterios para una política de integración popular* (Primera Semana Social de Chile, 1964), p. 219.
[29] Gabriel A. Almond and James S. Coleman, eds., *The Politics of the Developing Areas* (Princeton: Princeton University Press, 1960).
[30] Halperin, *op. cit.*, p. 27.

firm political tradition. On his side, Silvert states that "despite the work of many scholars, there is no generally accepted explanation of why Chile has developed into political patterns so different from its neighbors. Instead, the very fact that Chile's social weaknesses have been so intimately examined over the past half century had led to the opposite reaction—amazement that the profound poverty of so many Chileans has not produced massive political violence. At least part of the answer to this question is to be found in political ideas and behavior patterns."[31]

In the face of an objective revolutionary situation such as we have described, what meaning did this long democratic tradition have?

In the first place, it revealed that in the political structure of the state, despite its democratic formalism, there existed grave structural deficiencies and that the instrument state was inadequate to accelerate the process of economic and social development.

In the second place, the political traditions of the Chilean people reinforced the criterion that it was possible to bring about changes within the democratic scheme.

Only a complete analysis of the sociopolitical evolution of Chile would permit us to have a correct view of the reasons for disequilibrium between political stability and economic and social development, on the one hand, and the lack of efficiency of the instrument state, on the other. Unfortunately we cannot go deeply into the matter, and the shortcomings of a synthesis are very great.

But we can point out a few very clear facts.

1. As Professor Gil has very wisely indicated, the system of proportional representation, as it functioned until 1958, stimulated the fragmentation of parties.[32] For many years it was impossible to create a popular or legislative consensus over a concrete and integral plan of economic and social development.

[31] Silvert, op. cit., p. 86.
[32] Federico Gil, Los partidos políticos chilenos (Buenos Aires: Depalma, 1962), p. 52.

Confronted with executives who at times had a certain charisma, and who presented the electorate the beginning of programs that were never very well developed, congresses kept arising with generally opposing majorities.

2. The electorate, for various legal and regulatory reasons, remained very small until 1958. In 1952 women took part for the first time in a presidential election. Nevertheless, less than a million voters came to the polls. In 1958 a bit more than 1.2 million cast votes, and Jorge Alessandri was elected by a vote of 389,909.

Because of a new election law, sponsored by the PDC, in the presidential elections of 1964, 2.4 million voters participated, that is, an increase of 100 percent over the previous election. Frei was elected with 1,406,202 votes.

3. Conflicts between the President and Congress lacked a final arbiter, a situation that often provoked crises of paralyzation or compromise solutions generally contrary to the interests of development.

4. Lack of simultaneity in presidential and parliamentary elections sharpened the confrontations between the two powers due to the natural variations in the position of the electorate.

These shortcomings of the political system determined in considerable measure the incapacity of the instrument state to deal with underdevelopment, but they cannot be considered as the only causes of the lack of positive results from the actions of the state.

In 1964 the people of Chile had become conscious of the need for change. This is proved if we keep in mind that the alternative presented to the electorate was between two different roads of change and that the candidate of the status quo never had any chance of success. There existed an objective revolutionary situation; the people had become conscious of the need for change, and the changes that this situation demanded had to be swift and radical, that is to say, revolutionary. It is for this reason that the study of the political development of Chile necessarily involves an analysis of the revolutionary process.

And for this reason the PDC posed in 1964 the imperious necessity for a Revolution in Freedom. The PDC appears, then, as an important factor in the revolutionary process.

The young Conservatives of the decade of the thirties, university people for the most part—among whom we may note Bernardo Leighton, Manuel Garretón, Eduardo Frei, Radomiro Tomić, and Ignacio Palma—were inspired by new ideas, principally those of the Church in the social field and those of French and Belgian social and political thinkers. They promptly wished to bring new ideas into the political arena. The Conservative youth organization, *Flange Nacional,* which acted with great autonomy, very soon entered into conflict with the directive boards of the Conservative party. The youth organization wished to transform the social conscience and the political position of the party. By and by relations between the Conservative youth of *Falange Nacional* and the older leadership of the party became increasingly tense. As Frei tells us, "it was inevitable that these two existing tendencies within the Conservative party should reach a stage where they could no longer coexist: they had a very different way of interpreting and confronting problems. There was a difference not only of ideas but also of attitude and sensibility. Therefore, this latent disagreement led to a break. . . . That is how the *Falange Nacional* was born in 1938 after a period of gestation that had started in 1935."[33]

The Chilean Christian Democratic Movement started with a very small electoral basis. In 1941 the *Falange Nacional* received 3.44 percent of all valid votes. In 1945, 3.9 percent; and in 1949, only 2.9 percent. In 1961, it received 15.93 percent. In the parliamentary elections of March 1965 the PDC obtained 47 percent of the total vote. This percentage permitted the PDC to elect 82 representatives, or members, of the Chamber of Deputies, which has 147 members, and 12 senators (the Senate only elected 20 of its 45 members). The PDC retained one Senate

---

[33] Alberto Edwards and Eduardo Frei, *Historia de los partidos políticos chilenos* (Santiago de Chile: Ed. del Pacífico, 1949), p. 243.

seat from among those not up for reelection. This means that it has only 13 senators out of the total of 45.

This growth clearly disclosed the initial composition of the party, consisting only of a professional and university elite, and its slow growth until 1961, accelerated afterwards in the sectors of the middle class, country people, and workers. The party is particularly strong among women, young professionals, and technicians.

It should be pointed out that despite its slow electoral growth the PDC was from its beginning quite strong among the university sectors, where its ideology captures the sympathies of majority groups. Since 1954 (when the PDC held only four seats in Congress), the elections of the Student Federation of Chile (which covers all students of the state university), have been dominated by the PDC. During the last ten years the PDC with some exceptions, has also won the elections in the other seven public and private universities of Chile.

According to Professor Gil, "While . . . membership has been drawn extensively from the Catholic middle-class elements of the electorate, efforts have also been made to attract Protestants, agnostics, atheists, and Jews. . . . As a political 'union' aspiring to represent the Center and the mass of independents, the Chilean Christian Democrats are seeking something broader than a party in the customary sense."[34]

The election of Frei by an absolute majority in itself already indicated the presence of an element for some time absent in Chilean politics: the existence of a broad popular consensus with respect to a program of change, of modernization within the framework of democracy. That this was not a decision without an ideological basis, guided by the charisma of a candidate, was proved by the electorate in giving a voting majority to the candidates of the PDC in the congressional election of March 1965, held six months after the presidential election. That is to

[34] Federico Gil, The Political System of Chile (Boston: Houghton Mifflin, 1966), p. 274.

say, the awakening of the consciousness of the people shaped itself in the creation of a consensus in support of a revolutionary program.

How do you translate into the force of political development in Chile an ideology that has for its goal a communitarian society and whose basic elements are communitarianism and personalism?

Personalism determines the impulse to develop a human economy, put to the service of man, for all the inhabitants of the nation, not for a minority. Personalism places the state in its just position and compels it to obtain and protect the natural prerogatives of the person. Its entire organization has as its aim the satisfaction of the material and spiritual needs of the whole man. The conclusion is that what is required of an efficient instrument state is that it be able to satisfy the needs of the person and permit his integral development. The aim of the state will be the attainment of the common good.

Communitarianism indicates the necessity of protecting and analyzing the social dimension of the person within the community, of promoting in the social field the formation of communities as intermediaries between man and the state, and promoting in the economic field the appearance of a type of communitarian property.

Together, personalism and communitarianism carry within them an implicit rejection of liberal individualism or Marxist totalitarianism. Personalism and communitarianism permeate the Christian Democratic ideology. They pose the demands of political development through progammatic channels. Both concepts demand a high degree of social participation which the state will be called upon to promote and protect. Through multiple organizations the person may find means for his complete development.

To sum up, we may say that personalism and communitarianism demand the presence of an efficient instrument state to guide the development of a human economy in the service of the community and to frame its action with respect for the dignity of the human person. Both presuppose the existence of a conceptual model of development distinct from that offered by capitalism and Marxism. With this ideology the PDC traces a Program of Revolution in Freedom.

This Revolution in Freedom necessarily implies a process of political development, since it requires revolutionary changes in structures in order to develop rapidly the economy. Also it involves an entering into the depths of a political theory that creates the conceptual frame within which the process unfolds.

The most interesting aspects of political development involved in the Program of Revolution in Freedom are found in the measures of adequation of the instrument state which have been considered indispensable. To a great extent they are found incorporated in the Proposed Reform of the Political Constitution sent to the Congress on November 30, 1964.

The principles are the following:

1. broadening the electoral body, even to include illiterates;
2. establishment of a mechanism of direct consultation with the people, such as plebiscites in specified cases;
3. a measure of reform in popular representation and the establishment of conflict of interest between servants of private interests and those taking part in public enterprises;
4. rationalization of the structure and operation of public power.

Together with these measures there are many more included in the Program of Revolution in Freedom which undoubtedly will have a direct effect on the political development of Chile. We may cite, among others, the agrarian reform, the administrative reform, the urban reform, the educational reform, and an extraordinary plan of industrialization. With these it is reasonable to expect the possiblity of building the new institutions that definitely consolidate the various forms of total participation of the people in the political power, national wealth, and benefits of the culture.[35]

---

[35] See "Documentos," *Política y Espíritu* (October 1966), 96.

Other measures put forth by the Revolution in Freedom have had as an effect the establishment of a patrimonial tax, which constitutes a form of obtaining a principle of redistribution of income; the participation of the state in the property of the principal source of national wealth, the copper mines; a merciless war on inflation which has resulted in a remarkable reduction in the annual rate of price increases; a redistribution of income through a bold policy of fixing salaries; a policy of housing construction adequate for the needs of the nation; and other such measures.

Perhaps one of the most interesting developments in the present government's Program that will have a great effect on the creation of an authentic national community, final goal of all political development, is the so-called *Promoción Popular*. As President Frei assured the people in his First State of the Nation Address, in May 1965, "we believe that once the people have electoral power, it is indispensable that they have access to the other forms of power through appropriate channels. . . . The road to power organization. The crisis consists in that the majority of our people are disorganized, even from the unions' point of view. In Chile, as it is known, only 10 percent of salaried personnel are organized." That is, the road of popular integration is found in the organization of the people and not in a political hypertrophy of the State. In its essence, then, *Promoción Popular* is an effort to open to the people the channels for their organization in order that they may be representatives of themselves before the public powers. On this basis have been created thousands of neighborhood committees, farmers' centers, and such. In all this action the state is limited by a concept of subsidiarity, that is, to facilitate and promote popular organization, but not infiltrate or direct it.

The measures proposed by the PDC, based on its ideological concepts of communitarianism and personalism, provoke a curious comment from Ernst Halperin. "The concept of communitarianism," he states, "is extremely useful to the Christian Democratic party leaders because it enables them to justify essential points of their immediate program, which would otherwise appear to be purely pragmatic, as necessary steps toward the establishment of the communitarian system."[36] Actually, what has occurred is practically the opposite: the ideological bases of the PDC seem to have gone to the point òf indicating measures coinciding with the demands of reality. That would prove the realism of the ideology, not a hypocritical pragmatism.

Qualifications of a prophet are required to give assurance that the process underway will attain complete success and that all the programmatic goals will be won. But it is enough to have a superficial knowledge of the good sense of history of the Chilean people, of their capacity of reaction to an adequate stimulus, to have faith that the program has great possibilities of becoming implemented.

It is not for us to analyze here the difficulties the Program has found, especially in congressional action on the measures of implementation. In this respect it serves to recall what President Frei stated in his first message to Congress: "Just as there is freedom to legislate within the Constitution, there will be freedom to negotiate within the Program. Just as there is no liberty to go against the Constitution, it will not be possible to go against the Program."

The Program, then, is flexible, not dogmatic, and should permit a margin of negotiation, but not of compromise contrary to the proposed goals. The Program is committed to a policy of change and modernization, that is, to translating the real need of Chile. For this reason it is believed that the popular verdict, to which it is subject by ideological reasons, will continue being favorable.

Many questions remain pending, and will only be answered with the passage of time. The Chilean experiment is still open. For the first time in history a revolutionary process within democratic boundaries is being developed in Chile. The first ones to have a proud consciousness of this fact are the Chileans

[36] Halperin, op. cit., p. 198.

themselves. After all, as Maritain said, "the democracies bear in a fragile vessel the hopes of the world, I would say also the biological hopes of Mankind. And above all the vessel is very frail. . . . Democracy may be unpolished, clumsy, defective. Perhaps it merits severe judgment. However, democracy is the only road along which must travel the progressive energies of human history."

9: THE CHILEAN POLITICAL PROCESS
Federico G. Gil

In 1815 Simón Bolívar predicted in his famous Jamaica letter that Chile had the greatest chance of any of the Latin American republics to achieve liberty and progress. Although that prediction, as it befitted a romantic age, was somewhat quixotically based upon what the Liberator referred to as the "innocent customs and the virtues of its inhabitants,"[1] it nevertheless came partly true. The long years of orderly and stable government during the nineteenth century constituted Chile's most significant asset on the road to nationhood. In time Chile developed enlightened legal and political institutions that put it considerably ahead of the majority of the Latin American countries in political development. A political system has emerged in which legality is reflected, there is a fairly substantial measure of popular representation, and the three organs of government are each able to function without undue restraint from the others. The political climate is characterized by high standards of morality among political leaders, a fairly low degree of personalism, and, above all, full freedom of information of all ideological kinds and persuasions. In addition, the highly complex Chilean scene offers a good example of a strong and well-developed political party system. However, Chile has been weighted down by serious institutional and organizational handicaps and by seemingly insoluble socioeconomic maladjustments, which counterbalance the favorable conditions. Politically speaking, Chile is split into two segments: the approximately one-fifth of all Chileans who

[1] Jaime Eyzaguirre, *La fisonomía histórica de Chile* (Santiago, 1958), p. 96.

live under modern conditions and form the effective nation, and the large mass of underprivileged and uneducated people, alienated and excluded from the political process, who exist as a nation apart. To put it succinctly, one may use the words of Juan Bautista Alberdi and say, "Chile escaped disorder, but not backwardness." A keen observer of the Latin American scene, James Bryce, put it in even blunter terms when he wrote that Chile was "the prisoner of one hundred families."[2]

The survival of the monarchist and aristocratic traditions of colonial Chile after independence made it feasible to organize the country under a political system founded upon an authoritarian structure which did not rest arbitrarily upon forcible seizure of power or abusive use of this power. Gradually this system was to evolve into parliamentarism, at the same pace as the feudal-bourgeois oligarchy became stronger than the Presidents, until executive absolutism was defeated. Stability was achieved precisely because the colonial past had been preserved, but the price that was paid for order and peace was social backwardness.

The social transformation which permitted the passing from the stage of the "autocratic republic" (1830–1871) to the "liberal republic" (1871–1891) occurred with the emergence of a new mining and commercial bourgeoisie. This new class, conscious of its strength, played a significant role in the ensuing era of moderation during which the political system, although still far from party government, began to allow at least some participation of organized groups in national politics. Although far from being characterized by political liberty, the period witnessed the enactment of anticlerical laws and legislation extending suffrage to all Chilean males of twenty-five years of age and removing the income and property restrictions imposed by the Constitution of 1833.[3]

The War of the Pacific opened a new era of prosperity. The

[2] James Bryce, South America: Observations and Impressions (New York: Macmillan Co., 1912), p. 221.

[3] These reforms were introduced during the administration of President Domingo Santa María.

newly acquired wealth had repercussions in the structure of
society as well as in politics. Politically it served to assure continuing domination of the ruling class, but economically it was
the cause of an excessive dependence upon foreign markets
which produced a severe imbalance in Chile's internal economy.
In addition, this period marked the arrival of large foreign
investments.

The revolution of 1891, led by a rebellious Congress and presented to the nation as one to depose a tyrant who had placed
himself above the Constitution, gained the support of the
majority of the population. But there was no great social reform
involved in this conflict. Both sides in the Civil War of 1891
represented a single economic group split in a struggle for a
monopoly of political power.

President José Manuel Balmaceda's tragic death marked the
end of the old presidential omnipotence and the beginning of
the parliamentary republic (1891–1925), the period that has
been called "the futile years," during which government in
Chile reached its lowest ebb. A congressional oligarchy exer-
cised total power, while the masses remained indifferent to
administrative inefficiency and political corruption. Profound al-
terations, however, took place in the sociopolitical complex and
led to a great social and economic upheaval. The economic chaos
that followed the end of World War I's boom became the lever
for catapulting social problems into the political arena. Economic developments had integrated new and significant groups
into the middle class, an addition which contributed much new
substance and vigor to it. The restructuring brought about by
economic changes affected the lower class also. The northern
mineral wealth and the southern coal mines had given rise to
an awakening industrial proletariat. When the reaction in civic
spirit set in, public opinion was aroused and new segments of
the population began to demand a fundamental redistribution of
power. "Change had come swiftly—an industrial revolution and
social upheaval hand-in-hand—the machine, the proletariat, the
metropolis, and the intellectual middle class appearing almost

simultaneously on the scene."[4] Oligarchical domination collapsed, and riding the huge wave of discontent, Arturo Alessandri Palma, a champion of the common man, won a narrow victory in the presidential elections of 1920.

The frustrating years of attempted reforms, congressional obstruction, and military intervention were followed by significant institutional changes introduced by the Constitution of 1925, which provided for a strong executive and put an end to the parliamentary republic. Three features of the new constitutional system were a system of proportional representation, the selection of the President by the Congress if any candidate failed to receive a majority, and the separation of the dates of congressional and presidential elections. The first was in practice to encourage party fragmentation and unstable congressional coalitions. The second was to mean that in a multiparty system the President was often to owe his election to a parliamentary coalition with the consequent squabbles over patronage. The third led a changeable public opinion frequently to elect a President and a Congress hostile to one another.[5] The executive and legislative branches, as a result, were likely to represent a different coalescing of public opinion on varying issues, thus to create a natural antagonism between the two. Also, in the theory the new constitution turned away from the laissez-faire economic and Darwinistic social views of the past, to provide for state planning and governmental assumption of primary responsibility in social welfare matters.

A new political organization, the Communist party, destined to enjoy widespread support among the Chilean workers, appeared during Alessandri's first presidency, which ended three months before completion of his term. But some time later the four-year dictatorship of Carlos Ibáñez (1927–1931) forced all parties from the political arena. When public agitation and

[4] Federico G. Gil, *The Political System of Chile* (Boston: Houghton Mifflin, 1966), p. 56.
[5] *Ibid.*, p. 59.

economic depression brought the collapse of Ibáñez, there followed a period of fifteen months of political agitation and social unrest unequaled in the nation's history. A new military coup put an end to the "socialist republic" established by the group of military men and civilians led by Marmaduque Grove. The "social question" had become by then the crucial issue in Chilean politics, and after a decade of disorder and experiment there was need for a realignment of political forces.

The two essentially conservative parties, the Conservative and the Liberal, came out unscathed from the turmoil, with their economic base intact, because of their internal cohesiveness. Having now no issues to separate them, the two were destined to unite in a rightist bloc. The Radical party—of all Chilean parties the most broadly based, since it included a heterogeneous conglomeration of northern liberals from the mines, large and small southern landholders, and the petite bourgeoisie of professionals and bureaucrats—was now the stronghold of the urban middle class. It ceased being liberalism's extreme wing to become the spokesman of the middle masses and part of the proletariat. It played the role of moderating, or center, force within the new socioeconomic leftism. While the Radicals veered to the left, the first of the populist parties, the Democratic party (*Partido Demócrata*), slowly moved away from its original proletarian base and became a lower-middle-class organization. The newly born Chilean Left was now represented by the other two populist parties, the Communist and the Socialist.[6] In a short time another new group was to form, a new party destined to become in another three decades the dominant political force in Chile. The new *Falange Nacional*, inspired by the theories and philosophy emanating from the European Social Christian movements, later became the Christian Democratic party (PDC).

[6] Three other parties of relative importance appeared during this turbulent era of the 1930's: the leftist Radical Socialist, the center-right Agrarian party, and an offshoot of the Democratic party. In 1933 there emerged a Nazi group, the Nationalist Socialist movement of Chile.

The victory of the parties of the Left and Center in the 1938 election ushered in the Popular Front. For the first time in Chilean political history, middle-class and proletarian groups, well organized and pledged to basic ideological principles, challenged the traditional forces which had held a monopoly of power since independence. Also for the first time a President was elected predominantly by the middle and lower groups of society. However, the small margin of victory and the obstructionist rightist Congress did not produce the most propitious atmosphere for reform, and the Popular Front fell apart in 1941 after a series of internal struggles.

Between 1941 and 1958 Chile was governed by a system of coalition politics. A trend had finally crystallized into a definite alignment of political forces into three great blocs. The Radical party, the largest and broadest based, necessarily became the center of gravity of Chilean politics, and after the coalition of leftist forces in 1938 seized power from the aristocratic elite, it dominated this coalition for fourteen years, while within the ranks of the party two wings wrestled for supremacy. The schizophrenic personality of the Radicals, composed of one current which is leftist and Marxist-oriented and another which responds to traditional liberalism, served well to prevent dangerous extremism, but the effectiveness of government was bound to suffer. Also, the periodic Radical necessity to depend on rightist support permitted the Chilean plutocracy to recover at least part of the ground it had lost in 1938. Actually their base of power— namely, their hold on the rural parts of Chile—had remained untouched. At no time during the years of leftist coalition politics did the leadership attempt any reform involving the partition, expropriation, or even the increased taxation of the landed estates, and the *latifundio* system was left intact. No basic restructuring of society was ever undertaken.

Inflation, an increasing urbanization that multiplied the problems of city dwellers, slackening economic development during the later Radical years, and the popular belief that political parties were corrupt and that all politicians were self-seeking and venal resulted in 1952 in a remarkable victory for Ibáñez, the candidate who considered himself above politics. The impact of his election on the Chilean political system was important because it affected the voting habits of an important group of voters. The most significant thing about Ibáñez's victory is that for the first time the majority of rural workers and *inquilinos* (tenant farmers) defied the rightist landowners in order to vote for Ibáñez.

Like his Radical predecessors, Ibáñez began to rule with the support of left-wing parties but ended his administration with the support of the rightist parties. By the middle of the 1950's economic stagnation had overtaken Chile while population growth continued, agricultural production lagged, and the series of tariff-protected industrial booms played out as internal markets were satisfied. These were problems which could not be solved through the use of traditional parliamentary methods, but Ibáñez, despite his strong-man image, was unwilling to resort to drastic measures. He ended a lonely figure, deserted by all the political groups that had carried him to power. As the presidential election of 1958 approached, the political alignment included four indentifiable broad groupings: the Conservatives and Liberals together making their strongest bid for power since 1938; the Christian Democrats, appealing to intellectuals, technicians, and non-Marxist leftists, as well as Catholics; the leftist coalition known as Popular Action Front (*Frente de Acción Popular*, or FRAP), fortified by the unification of the Socialists; and the Radicals, who, unable to enlist the support of independent leftists, found themselves isolated for the first time.

The rightist forces, led by Jorge Alessandri, enjoyed a slim victory in 1958. Yet even if they were willing to concede the need for social reform, they remained generally committed to the past and proved unable to carry out the radical alternatives demanded by Chilean society. In 1961 the Radical party joined the Conservative-Liberal alliance, and in 1963 the three parties constituted the Democratic Front (*Frente Democrático*). Discontent was general and pressures grew stronger for adjustments in the political system during the Alessandri administration. Significant developments of the early 1960's were the impressive gains made by the FRAP coalition and by the Christian Democrats. There could be clearly detected a strong shift of the electorate toward the moderate and extreme Left in the congressional and municipal elections of 1961 and 1963, respectively. The leftist coalition continued to make inroads in the rural areas, which were traditionally the stronghold of the Conservatives. In 1963 the Christian Democrats, because of their success in attracting new voters, particularly the women, became the nation's largest major party. While in 1950 it had received only 4.7 percent of the vote, in the 1963 municipal elections it led all other parties by being given 23 percent of the vote.

This victory was shortly followed by the even more spectacular Christian Democratic triumph of 1964. Their presidential candidate, Eduardo Frei, achieved what no other Chilean President in this century had done by accumulating an absolute majority of the vote. Trailing behind were FRAP's candidate Salvador Allende and Radical Julio Durán.[7] Among the most important factors contributing to this unprecedented victory was the issue of Communism ably exploited by the Christian Democrats and the extraordinary appeal and attractiveness of Frei and his program.

The significance of the election for the Chilean political system was essentially its strengthening effect on national political integration by drastically altering the past pattern of political socialization and recruitment. Over one-half of the electorate who voted in 1964 had never voted before for a Chilean President.

The attitude patterns which are inculcated into the citizen through the socialization process vary directly in Chile in relation to his social class. For all intents and purposes, the average *inquilino*, or tenant farmer, lives in another world from that of the middle- or upper-class Chilean. Traditionally he has been

[7] For an analysis of this election see Federico G. Gil and Charles J. Parrish, *The Chilean Presidential Election of September 4, 1964* (Washington, D.C.: Institute for the Comparative Study of Political Systems, 1965).

separated from the polity by a political as well as a social chasm. The pattern of socialization under the *fundo* system is one which discourages the development of politically relevant attitudes. Furthermore, leftist political groups in Chile, until recently, were essentially urban oriented. They rarely attempted to seek support in the rural areas because they viewed them as the bulwark of the Chilean Right. In general, the average urban Chilean has not been willing to launch a frontal attack on the *fundo* system to gain political objectives.

Of the changes that have taken place in the last decades in the Chilean political process, perhaps the most important is the transformation of these traditional attitude patterns of rural Chile. High-pressure campaigns in the rural areas urging the *inquilino* to vote for a change in the system under which they have had gratifying results for the Left and Center-Left parties. The fact that his vote is now being sought, and that the two national political organizations now attempting to recruit the rural Chilean into the system are both strongly in favor of agrarian reform, portends many significant changes still to come. Peasant support went first to Ibáñez in 1952, but in recent years it has aided FRAP and the Christian Democrats more than other groups. However, the mere act of voting independently, while it is a first step, is not sufficient. There is need of creating those intermediary structures capable of providing a way to express demands and to bring effective pressure on the political decision-makers during the time between electoral periods. The Christian Democrats' emphasis on the *Promoción Popular* program, designed to integrate the urban and rural poor into the political system, indicates a new awareness that such structures will become important sources of party strength.

Another important change in Chilean politics since the end of World War II has been the result of shifts away from the working class and toward the middle and upper segments in the distribution of the national income. One political implication of this phenomenon has been the large increase in popular support for extreme Left and Center-Left political parties.

In this century Chile evolved a political system based principally on a balance between a traditional upper class and a burgeoning middle class.[8] The urban proletariat and the rural workers were originally excluded from effective political roles. Since the 1920's the urban working class has been given some access to and participation in the political process, but their new political role has failed to bring them many substantial economic gains, although this does not mean that it has not obtained some rewards. Nevertheless, social security benefits, for example, are enjoyed by the working class, but these benefits are at a lower level than those received by other groups. This unequal share in economic benefits has in political terms meant increasing support given by working-class voters to the parties of the extreme Left and more recently to the Christian Democratic party. Much of the social-welfare legislation that has been adopted in the past favored middle-class groups specifically.[9]

Another recent important change in Chilean politics has been the increase in the electorate. The politicization of the rural worker since 1952 accounts for only a part of this increase. Electoral reforms introduced in 1958 and 1960 to establish easier registration procedures as well as stronger penalties for abstention from voting are also partly responsible for the increase in voting. But perhaps even more important than the growth of the rural vote has been the rise in the female vote. In 1964, 54.7 percent of the voters were women. All these factors combined meant that in the 1964 presidential election over one-half of those voting were casting their ballots for the first time in their lives.

Significant developments have affected the complexion of the Chilean party system in the last decade. Many small parties have disappeared from the scene, and those surviving have

[8] See John J. Johnson, *Politics of Change in Latin America: The Emergence of the Middle Sectors* (Stanford: Stanford University Press, 1958) and Federico Gil, *The Political System of Chile.*

[9] See David Félix, "Chile," in Adamantios Pepelasis, Leon Mears, and Irma Adelman, eds., *Economic Development* (New York: Harper & Row, 1961).

joined blocs. The Radical party, which held the key to coalition politics as leaders or partners of Center-Left and Center-Right alliances, was dislodged by the Christian Democratic party from its long-held monopoly of the Center as representative of the professional and worker middle-class elements. However, the polarization of the electorate which took place in the 1964 presidential elections has subsisted only in some respects. The rightist forces as represented by the Conservative and Liberal parties, weakened by fatal political setbacks in recent years, have recently joined forces with other conservative groups to found a new political organization, the National party (PN). On the left, continuance of FRAP seems to disprove the tradition of disarray and bitter rivalries which have plagued the history of Chilean leftism. Unity has paid handsomely for the two principal partners in the FRAP coalition, for their electoral strength and political influence have risen to new heights during the 1960's. The Radical party, displaced as the representative of the urbanite middle-class and labor elements by the Christian Democrats and split between traditionalists and modernists, is following at present an uncertain and swerving path.

Finally, there is another phenomenon that has remained with Chilean politics and has been analyzed elsewhere.[10] It is the essentially anomic appeal (emotional, nationalistic, and antipolitical) which has recurred from time to time in the political process. Both Ibáñez in 1952 and Alessandri in 1958 were elected as men above politics, striving for "national," rather than "political," solutions to the nation's problems. The rise of this kind of anomic appeal has probably been the result partly of the periodic disillusionment with party politics and partly of the economic grievances felt by almost all sectors of the population. This nationalistic appeal that emphasizes the emotional and antipolitical was at its height during Ibáñez's campaign in 1952, but when his administration turned out to be weak and ineffective, the party system was restored to pub-

---

[10] Federico G. Gil and Charles Parrish, op. cit., pp. 14–17.

lic confidence. It is possible, if the present drive for reforms
fails or if the Christian Democratic administration proves ineffective in dealing with Chile's problems, that there may be a
resurgence of this disillusionment with the consequent rise of
antipolitical, nationalistic appeals.

The accession to power of a party committed to a highly
developed political ideology with deep spiritual roots after the
long period of Radical rule is likely to have a substantial impact
upon the political system. Radical dependence on coalition government, with its fragmentation of purpose and method, inevitably resulted in vague and undefined ideology and hollow
and expedient programs. The most, and perhaps the only, consistent feature of Radical philosophy has been its reliance on
improving the lot of the lower segments of Chilean society by
evolutionary methods rather than by revolutionary ones. On the
other hand, the Revolution in Freedom advocated by the Christian Democrats might be a peaceful revolution, but it is, nevertheless, a revolution. Christian Democratic acceptance of the
need for at least a restricted form of class struggle implies the
need of encouraging the masses to obtain the means of giving
their demands a political articulation.[11] Only then will the
masses be in a position to secure from the privileged groups
those fundamental changes that ordinarily these groups will not
be willing to accept. What could have greater effects than the
enlargement of the opportunities of the dispossessed, excluded
until now from any access to the political machine, and the
incorporation of all available social elements into the national
community? It is, then, logical to expect that important changes
will occur in the next few years which may affect all phases of
the political process.

In addition to those transformations in the pattern of political behavior which have been described already, there are others
that are only beginning to emerge. Substantial changes may be
in the making toward the democratization and modernization

[11] Frederick B. Pike, *Chile and the United States, 1880–1962* (Notre Dame:
University of Notre Dame Press, 1963), p. 260.

of political structures through proposed constitutional reforms that are designed to give the President authority to resort to the people directly concerning fundamental measures. Constitutional reforms submitted to the Congress by President Frei in 1965 have yet to be approved in whole except for the provisions related to the right of property. However, new governmental structures have been created, such as the Ministry of Housing and the Central Planning Office (ODEPLÁN) attached to the presidency. Less formal structures have also developed, such as the *Consejería de Promoción Popular*, which is entrusted with integrating the urban and rural poor into effective political roles and is supported with funds from the executive branch. New labor organizations of importance have emerged among the rural elements, although the industrial unions, for the most part, have remained outside the influence of the Christian Democratic revolution.

A significant departure is also noticeable at present in the traditional approach to governmental problems. There is a disposition on the part of the present administration to deal with national problems by taking into account all social, economic, and political aspects of each issue through the comprehensive planning of all national activities within an ideological context. Regardless of the relative ambiguity of such terms as the "communitarian society" and "economic humanism" there is nevertheless an ideological commitment and an essential belief in social pluralism and political democracy. Furthermore, there exists a consensus that the mobilization of all disposable resources is essential, though there remain differences concerning what are the most effective methods of achieving such mobilization. Complementing the comprehensive planning approach, the government is assuming responsibility for such new functions as promoting unionization and incorporating marginal segments of the population into society, a task which carries with it the assumption by the government of additional financial responsibilities.

The political style utilized by the party in power is characteristic of the politics of modernization with its emphasis upon innovation. Efforts to develop a system of communications, designed to reach the entire population, through the use of all modern media as well as organizational efforts to engage as representative a cross section as possible of social groups in the service of a "national cause" are being pursued with vigor amidst charges of totalitarianism proffered by the opposition.

This new political style is at least in part a product of the peculiar conditions in which the PDC finds itself as the only political party since 1925 with an absolute majority in the Chamber of Deputy but with minority representation in the Senate. But it is also a consequence of the Christian Democrats' determination to preserve their ideological purity by closing the door to alliances with any other party or group of parties. The most important measures of the administration during the last two years have been concerned with anti-inflationary policies, the "chileanization" of foreign investments, constitutional reforms, agrarian reform, education, *Promoción Popular*, labor organizations, and, in the realm of foreign affairs, the development of trade relations with all countries, including those of the Communist bloc. Ideological differences among the opposition parties concerning these measures has greatly contributed to facilitate the independent position of the PDC and the maintenance of the nonalliance principle, since it made it possible for the party to obtain, on some occasions, the support of the rightist elements and, at other times, that of the leftist groups, depending on the nature of the question at issue.

Lastly, references are being made today by some observers to a possible revival of parliamentarism. To some the temptation to compare the present situation with the 1891 conflict between the executive and congressional branches of the government is too strong to resist. This comparison, in our opinion, is not valid. For one thing, the experiment of 1891 was in effect an attempt to operate a parliamentary government without parties, or at least without parties that acted on real problems. It could be characterized as the development of trustee government to hold things together at a moment when there was no ready and available channel through which political action could be directed into constructive action.[12] The present situation, frustrating as it is for a chief executive continuously harassed by the obstructionist tactics of the Senate, has nothing in common with the 1891 crisis. This is not to deny that there is not a strong tradition of congressional independence arising from the period of the parliamentary republic. Executive omnipotence has never been an unrelieved fact in Chile except in times of constitutional subversion. It is equally true that the programs of the rightist parties and of the Radicals have consistently proposed constitutional reforms aimed at the establishment of a modified parliamentary system whenever circumstances permit. However, the recent attempt to give the chief executive authority to dissolve Congress, a power generally featured in parliamentary regimes, without the vesting of ample powers in the legislature, along with other constitutional reforms, could tend, if anything, to strengthen presidential authority. Perhaps if what is sought is to prevent sterile conflicts between a President and a Congress and the consequent impasse in the road to reform, a much more effective way would be to hold at the same time both presidential and congressional elections.

To sum up, politically Chile, as every observer has noted, possesses a series of characteristics normally ascribed to highly developed countries and a reserve of political maturity and social patience. In a troubled continent much has already been accomplished to make Chile a unique example of progress. Only a country with such assets could have withstood the very serious economic maladjustments it has experienced without falling into political disaster and social chaos. As for the future, it is fair to conclude, then, that further political development in this nation would depend essentially upon the successful incorporation of all social segments into the political process in time to adjust the rising demands of the lower levels of society to the requirements of future economic growth.

[12] Kalman H. Silvert, Chile: Yesterday and Today (New York: Holt, Rinehart & Winston, 1965), pp. 68–69.

INDEX

187